$1.00

The Starduster

The Starduster

Norm Weis

Prentice-Hall, Inc., Englewood Cliffs, New Jersey

Printed in the United States of America
Prentice-Hall International, Inc., London
Prentice-Hall of Australia, Pty, Ltd., Sydney
Prentice-Hall of Canada, Ltd., Toronto
Prentice-Hall of India Private Ltd., New Delhi
Prentice-Hall of Japan, Inc., Tokyo
Prentice-Hall of Southeast Asia Pte. Ltd., Singapore
Whitehall Books Limited, Wellington, New Zealand
10 9 8 7 6 5 4 3 2 1

Library of Congress Cataloging in Publication Data

Weis, Norman D
    The starduster.

SUMMARY: The author relates how he finally realized
his dream of building his own plane and learning to fly
it in competition.
    2. Weis, Norman D.   2.   Airplanes, Home-built.
3.   Air pilots—United States—Biography.   [1. Weis,
Norman D.   2.   Air pilots.   3.   Airplanes, Home-built]
I. Title.
TL540.W39A37   629.13'092'4   [B]   [92]   80-11068
ISBN 0-13-842914-6

For Bill Riedesel,
and for all others who cherish
the privilege of flight.

With special thanks to
Mike Herbison
Scott Jones
Dick Reitz
Joe Stewart

Contents

1/First Flight

A third-quarter moon cast faint light on the little biplane perched incongruously on my driveway. The moonlight bounced crescents from each rib-rise along the scalloped upper wing and gave outline to the propeller and the rake of the fuselage.

It seemed almost like a large model airplane, capable of flight, perhaps, but surely unable to carry a man aloft. Six steps could span its wings and an arm stretch enfold its tail. But the image was deceptive. This was a machine of freedom, a machine that could carry a man beyond the clouds, that would feel no tether of time or fetter of schedule.

Three years of my life were invested in this little plane. In its frame of wood and metal rode a thousand dreams. On this day, the two of us would taste that freedom and seek those dreams.

I had flown before, perhaps a thousand hours, but never in such frisky company. This craft was far smaller than anything I had flown and carried more horsepower per pound of total weight than any plane in my experience. Its sensitivities would tax my pilotage, perhaps exceed it. My rusty skills were only recently renewed and readied for the effort. I had practiced in a tricky Luscombe and had mastered its obstinate rudder, making repeated takeoffs and landings with the controls trimmed both to full nose up and full nose down to prepare myself. I was as ready as I could be, and I hoped the plane was also ready. My life would depend on its structural integrity, and that integrity was of my own making.

Dawn was drawing a thin line along the eastern horizon as I fussed over the plane, feeling its line and form, mentally checking each vital bolt, nut, cotter pin and safety wire. A sudden shaft of sunlight brought color to the red and blue trim. The white-lettered STARDUSTER on the nose blazed forth. The plane took on charm and personality. She *was* a beauty!

The deputy sheriff arrived on schedule, followed in short order by a few friends, all flying enthusiasts. The Starduster's tail wheel was quickly replaced with a trailer hitch, and the hitch attached to a pickup truck. In a thoroughly undignified manner, the little biplane began its reluctant trip to the airport, tail high and backward.

We threaded our way past darkened homes and along empty streets, then entered a little-used winding field road. The deputy led, all lights flashing. Half a dozen cars followed behind, each driver sworn to stop any rear approaching vehicle at the expense of his own.

Because the gate leading to the main road was too narrow by a previously-measured six inches, the loose end-post had to be removed and the Starduster unhitched and carefully eased through. Some of the crew reinstalled the gate post. Others gently hauled the Starduster's 800 pounds into position on the main road to recouple with the pickup. It was a straight route to the highway and a short mile further to the County Airport.

The sun was up and warming the ground when the caravan came to a stop in front of the big pink hangar. Willing hands unhitched the plane and helped reinstall the tail wheel. The Starduster once again assumed a perky three-point stance, all signs of reluctance gone. Now she was eager for flight.

A small crowd had gathered, watching while I made the final

2

inspection. This would be a bad time to overlook the obvious.

Fuel: 10 gallons of 80/87.
Drain cocks: dewatered and checked for sediment.
Oil: to the mark, 7 quarts of 50 weight.
Controls: free, solid and checked for nuts and safeties.
Cowl: all fasteners secured.
Flying wires: all eight tight and safetied at each end, and each one tuned to middle C.
Chute: in place, all straps laid out for easy entrance.
Auxiliary power unit: plugged in, ready for start-up.

Everything was ready. I stepped to the wing walk, and climbed into the seat. If I had been showing any swagger, it was erased when, as I eased my feet into position, I ran the control stick cold up my pant leg. Damn! I made a brave show of checking the mags, carb heat, throttle and mixture, while discreetly extricating the stick.

"CLEAR!"

Several voices answered, "Clear."

The engine started on the third turn. With the power cord detached, I taxied to the ramp, confident that all was checked and ready. But the tower failed to answer my call: Either I was not transmitting or was unable to receive. Downcast, I taxied back and shut down.

A conference ensued. The lack of a clicking sound when the stick-mounted mike switch was depressed indicated a break in the switch wire, and that wire was under the floorboards.

Twenty minutes later I located the break. The wire had separated in the middle of a soldered connection. Such connections cannot stand vibration. I thought I had corrected all of my earlier mistakes, but this one had been overlooked. I wondered if I had overlooked anything else. The thought was unnerving.

A solderless coupling and squeezer were passed into the cockpit and the repair completed. The stick switch again sent a click to the earphones, and the tower responded quickly to a test call. The radio transmitted well and the reception seemed adequate.

With the multitude of chute straps, shoulder straps and

seat belts again latched and tightened, I briefly checked the cockpit and instrument panel.

"CLEAR!"

Again the answer: "Clear."

But now the engine wouldn't start. Flooded perhaps. With half throttle it still refused to start. After several shots of prime the engine still failed to fire, and the battery was getting weak. Faintly, through the padded helmet, I heard someone shout, "Turn your mags on." With that small oversight rectified, the engine roared to life. This was getting to be embarrassing.

"Casper ground, this is Starduster One November Whiskey at hangar 5. May I make some taxi tests on the ramp?"

"Starduster One November Whiskey. That's affirmative."

At slow speeds she handled beautifully. Not a sign of the rudder lag so common to larger taildraggers. No feel of being behind the motion, like an auto sliding in mud. Punch the left rudder, and you go left, quicker and further than expected. Right rudder the same. Thanks to the foresight of early airplane builders, every control movement was directionally appropriate. Push the stick forward and you literally push the nose down. Pull it back and the nose rises. Push the throttle forward, you go forward. All the motions come naturally, provided one has no earlier bias. As a youngster I had tried to learn aircraft control movements sitting on a sled with a hammer upended as a stick. It was difficult because I knew how to run a sled, and its control was opposite to that of an aircraft. Once I had overcome this obstacle, I could practice every maneuver in my twenty-five-cent book, *How to Fly.*

The rudder was comfortable now. Its sensitivity was delightful. I caught myself grinning foolishly. I swung the plane around for a 360 or two, then faced the control tower, still grinning.

"Casper ground. I'd like to make a few runs down the ramp at medium speed, say 40 miles an hour."

"That's affirmative."

Rudder control at the faster speed was positive, and a bit quicker, requiring new accommodation. The nose moved back and forth in quick jerks, exactly imitating my overcontrolling foot

4

movements. By the second run I had the hang of it. I was able to taxi straight and true with the tail wheel clear of the ground. I requested permission to make a few high-speed runs down the ramp and received another affirmative.

My communications with ground control were broadcast from loudspeakers along the flight line. It was a standard procedure. There is no privacy on aviation frequencies. Pilots warming their engines or flying in the area could hear both sides of the conversation on their aircraft radios. Knots of onlookers gathered about the loudspeakers. A plane about to taxi by pulled off to watch.

With full throttle, the plane accelerated rapidly. I held mild forward pressure on the stick to bring the tail up. It rose slowly, stabilized, then rose drastically before I could back off. The propeller came within an inch of chewing the blacktop. On the second try the tail over-rose again, but I managed to catch it sooner. I assumed that the elevator control was simply more sensitive than expected, and that I would learn its proper handling with practice, as I had the rudder. That was a dangerous assumption.

On the next run I let the speed build to 60 mph. I caught the tail over-rise with back pressure, and the plane became suddenly light on its wheels. It felt good and I couldn't help grinning. As the plane slowed, I keyed the mike, "Boy, she really wants to fly." Then I caught myself and added, "Casper ground, would this be an auspicious moment to give her a try?"

"Starduster One November Whiskey. What kind of a moment did you have in mind?"

"I mean, are we free of airliners? Are there any due in or out?"

"Negative. Taxi to runway three four, wind three two zero at ten knots, altimeter three zero zero two."

It was nearly two miles down the taxi ramp to runway 34. I had time to think as I zigzagged along.

Other pilots had tested other craft. My test of Starduster Whiskey would not be greatly different. I had studied the procedures at length and knew what to look for. Perhaps I didn't deserve to tease myself with the title "Test Pilot." This was no high-performance jet. There were no crash trucks at runway midpoint, no ejection seat, and my clothing was far from fireproof. On the other hand, if I were any kind of a test pilot, maybe I would have been smart enough to have seen to some of these precautions.

There was one big item in my favor though. The test pilot pits his skill against the possible imperfections of a thousand factory workers and half a hundred aeronautical engineers. But the homebuilder is his own riveter, his own welder, his own fabric man and his own engine mechanic. He need not be concerned with the unknown quality of others' work. His worry is strictly his own.

I wondered how the plane would feel in the air. Would it need a great angle of attack to achieve a climb, as the old Fleet biplane did? Or would it be, as a friend described his first solo flight in a Pitts, "like strapping on a pissed-off bumblebee." I hoped for the latter.

I reached the threshold of runway 34 and, with brakes locked, ran the engine to 1,500 rpm. Left and right magnetos dropped the revolutions per minute by 50 each: normal. At full throttle, rpms reached 2,200, and dropped 150 with carburetor heat: again normal. Oil temperature and pressure were in the green. Controls were free. Trim was set at mid-travel. I switched to tower frequency.

"Casper Tower. Starduster One November Whiskey Experimental ready to go on three four."

"Starduster One November Whiskey. Hold for aircraft on half-mile final."

I watched the Cessna 150 slide in for a landing, its occupants glancing frequently at Starduster Whiskey. Everybody loves a biplane, especially one on its maiden flight.

"Starduster One November Whiskey. Cleared for takeoff."

NOW! On the center line, ease into full throttle. Tail is up. Watch out for over-rise. Ease off the forward pressure. Watch the rudder. Stay on the center line. Check the air speed. A quick glance shows 60. Back pressure and she's off and climbing. Speed now 90. More back pressure and the climb steepens to an unbelievable angle. She's a hot one—maybe not in the bumblebee class, but lively, very lively. We climb at 90 mph, gaining 1,500 feet per minute. A quick motion of the stick right and left, and instantly the wings rock 30 degrees each way. Sensitive! We reach 600 feet, pattern altitude, time for a 90-degree turn left, then a 45 right to exit the area. Two small moves with stick and rudder, and the turns are accomplished. The plane has reached an altitude of twelve hundred feet above the ground in less than a minute. I can't stop grinning. She's everything I had hoped for. Quick, sensitive, superb climber and capable of any maneuver I might dare to try. No longer will I look up with envy at other aircraft flown by other pilots. From now on the sky is mine!

But something is wrong. With throttle reduced to cruise, the Starduster wants to dive sharply. The hands-off flight I had hoped for is not to be. Even with full nose-up trim, strong back pressure on the stick is required to hold a level attitude. At reduced throttle, more back stick is needed, leaving precious little for maneuvering. I twist about to look at the tail surfaces. The elevator is riding high in the up position. The stall tests are alarming. At an indicated 75 mph, she sits and mushes and porpoises. There is no stall and there should be. Perhaps I should have sensed a problem when the tail over-rose during taxi tests.

I continue with "stall" tests, power on, power off, in various attitudes, recording the results on a pad taped to my right leg. The figures are not encouraging. Landing will be a bit of a problem. Various glide speeds show that 90 is barely safe. It feels much more controllable at 100. I decide to make a wheel landing, approach hot and touch down at a speed between 100 and 110 mph.

"Casper Tower, Starduster One November Whiskey, five miles west for landing."

"Starduster Whisk—runway m—." The sound coming through the earphones is overwhelmed by the engine and slip-stream. I duck my head deep in the cockpit to minimize the noise. "Say again?" After three tries I am still unable to read their transmission. "Casper Tower. I can't read you. I'll enter left down wind for three four. I have a nose-heavy condition. Hope you can clear the traffic."

I turn the radio off and concentrate on the landing. If I can only get her down without damage, it will be a simple matter to adjust the center of gravity and cure the nose-down tendency. Approaching at 130, carrying 2,400 rpm, I reduce power only slightly as the ground nears. Three feet above the ground at 120, it is still necessary to hold back pressure to maintain level flight. The ground races by much too fast, but there is no choice. I lower carefully, feeling for the ground. Lower. A tight squeal, and wheels make contact. Quickly I relax some of the back pressure in order to maintain contact. The little biplane rolls down the runway at well over 100 mph. With throttle retarded, the speed deteriorates and the tail slowly lowers to three-point.

The landing had been far easier than expected. It had been exciting and almost pleasant, with positive control throughout. In spite of the weight and balance problem, Starduster Whiskey was a gentle, forgiving creature.

The thrill of the flight was with me as I taxied in. The wide grin was back and could not be suppressed. I recalled the magic of my first flight in a light plane, and the sharp freedom I had felt on my first solo. Something happens to your soul when you fly alone for the first time. But to fly in a craft of your own making is an experience that rises to another order of magnitude. Twenty years of living without flying, and three years of building and dreaming, had culminated in this euphoric moment. Bellerophon, having mastered Pegasus, could have felt no more.

I taxied back along the ramp, aglow with pride, returning stares with a grin and a wave, knowing well that every pilot on the line would have given his right arm to fly this little sweetheart.

2/Tilting at
a New Windmill

When you are young there is small reason to look ahead, for life in that direction is endless. There is time enough for everything, and planning is unnecessary. Desires, passions, joy and sadness arrive and depart fortuitously.

Middle age brings a little more perspective. This is a time for holding on to the feeling of youth and pointedly ignoring the aging process, even while looking ahead far enough to increase your life insurance. But of course you still have every intention of living forever.

At the age of fifty, however, the future can no longer be ignored. Its finite nature is obvious. You're numerically on the downhill side of life. But there is one advantage: Now life can be judged with more certainty. Now you know that if there is still something you want to do, there is no longer a world of time in which to act.

When I was fifty and took a hard look ahead, I could see a

dozen more years of teaching, a dozen summers' backpacking, fishing and working on one project or another. Retirement would simply change the emphasis. The future looked pleasant and secure but devoid of any new adventure.

My early years had been full of surprise and discovery. Now, in retrospect, those years seemed more exciting than any of my plans for the future. Somewhere I had given up old delights and taken to more conservative pursuits. Like many of those around me, I had become a spectator rather than a participant. Now, perhaps, was my last chance to grasp life and bend it to my purpose. It was time to tilt at a new windmill.

I inventoried the past, looking for clues—pursuits worthy of repetition, endeavors that circumstance had brought to an early end, dreams that were never realized.

As a youngster, I had spent almost every Saturday with my best buddy, messing around at the Omaha Municipal Airport. My mother deplored such excursions, explaining that a nine-year-old had no business being two miles away from home. I countered by saying that my pal's mom said he could go. He used the same excuse. Being the middle child of the family of five youngsters proved quite an advantage. Mother had trouble keeping track of the boys, spending most of her time monitoring the two younger sisters. My father, a young Methodist minister, was far too occupied with church affairs to worry about his number-three son. Only the most flagrant violation brought his guiding hand into play, but on those rare occasions, the guiding hand usually held a thick leather razorstrap. It was a good thing my exploits were largely undiscovered, or my mom's problems would have been compounded, and my backside would have been sore with a far greater frequency.

When the first airliner with a flush toilet arrived in Omaha, my buddy and I were the first to flush it—right on the ramp. (We were thrown off the airport.) Twice the local grocer caught me stealing coupons from the tops of Thompson's Malted Milk cans. Each coupon could be sent in for a large picture of an airplane. A dozen of them lined the walls of my attic room. My buddy had fourteen.

But mostly we did harmless things. On our visits to the airport we spent hours standing around airplanes looking wistful, hoping to be invited for a ride. It never worked. At best we were permitted to sweep floors and empty buckets of used oil behind the hangars.

The two of us were consumed with a love of airplanes. We read everything available concerning flying machines. The sound of an approaching plane would send us tearing outside for a look. We could identify them all. If there was any doubt, we would call it a Stinson. None of our peers dared challenge our vast knowledge.

When the big Air Show came to Omaha, I was wild with excitement. I had tried to save my money, but the Depression made it difficult. My five-cents-a-week allowance, plus pin money from carrying groceries, did not add up to the price of a ticket.

My buddy and I, along with several dozen other kids in like circumstances, sneaked into the show by crawling under the woven wire fence. We were ejected—several times—but just as repeatedly sneaked back in. We missed a lot of the show running between access points, but the parts we saw were fantastic.

A fellow jumped out of a plane, way up high, wearing a black coverall with black webs between his legs and under his arms. He "flew" as he fell, doing flips and turns, then opened his parachute at the last moment.

A big brown balloon full of hot smokey air drifted upward and a man fell out—but he, too, had a parachute. The bag turned upside down and shot out a big cloud of black smoke.

Then a shiny two-winger took to the air and began doing things I had never seen before. He even did some things I had never even read about. His name, SPEED HOLMAN, was printed on the side of his airplane, and he could fly it upside down just as well as right side up. He could loop, roll over and fly sideways, one right after the other. I watched, totally enthralled. When Speed Holman landed, he had completely replaced Lindbergh as my personal hero.

Flying the Atlantic was all right, but this was something else. I ached to do the same stunts. My world would be complete if I could ever learn to fly like Speed Holman—maybe even get to where my stunts were good enough to keep a whole crowd of people on the ground spellbound.

We were kicked out again when Speed flew his second bunch of stunts. I didn't learn until later that he dove into the

11

ground upside down and was killed. They said he just got too close to the ground. He was still my hero, and in my mind he would always be just as I saw him last—looping, rolling and flying sideways.

Model building became my next great passion. I built scale models of boats and trains and airplanes—but mostly airplanes. I delighted in following the flight of the simplest glider, especially when the touchdown came with gentle kissing touch. Rubber-powered craft, weeks in the building, often carried my hopes to new extremes of exhilaration and frustration as they briefly flew, then crashed. My first gas-powered model plane had a wingspread of nearly five feet. It weighed so much more than my previous models that I doubted its ability to fly. It hung from the ceiling for weeks while I admired its upsweeping wing, its glossy red finish, piano wire landing gear and miniature balloon tires. One calm day, curiosity at a peak, I launched it by hand into tall grass. It tracked straight and true without a trace of stall or turn. The time had come to risk powered flight.

I wished that I were small enough to ride along. I knew the control movements by heart. If the plane dove, I could pull back on the stick and save it from a crash, or if it banked too steeply, I could give it help with a push to the side on the stick along with a quick jab on the rudder—if only I could ride along.

I put two full eyedroppers of gas in the tank and started the little engine. Faced into the light breeze, the plane trembled and surged in my hands, the wheels vibrating against the ground. I released it gently. The tail rose, and after a short run the plane lifted, tracing a gentle curve to the left. It climbed and became small with height. I ran, trying to stay underneath, praying that it would run out of gas. The buzz of the engine stopped suddenly, and the plane began to glide, banking gently to the right. I stood, turning in slow circles, watching it feel its way through small bumps of rough air. It passed over the road, turned full circle, closed with the ground, bounced, and rolled gloriously whole and free onto the road.

There were many other models: seaplanes, float planes, biplanes, canards, boom tails and conventional aircraft. Some failed to fly after repeated adjustments; others flew well, too well at times. One model landed in the open bed of a pickup traveling down the highway and was never seen again. Another caught in a thermal and flew unpowered for more than an hour before going out of sight. Later, a farmer returned a mangled engine and landing gear, all that had survived the trip through his cornpicker.

Later my life became filled with other pursuits: canoeing, kayaking and sailboating. But even while running with full spinnacker before a brisk wind, the sound of an engine overhead would always pull my attention skyward.

In my twenties I embraced flying again, but this time with the real thing. I found that flying full-sized aircraft added new dimensions to my understanding of flight. The view from inside an aircraft was totally different from the modeler's view of flight from the ground. Inside an airplane the plane's motion seemed to disappear; it was the horizon that moved, tilting right and left, rising and falling. Only at low level was the speed more noticeable and the track of the plane through the air more apparent.

Mild aerobatics put the hemispheres of the sky and earth in wild alternation. In time I learned the trick of "seeing" the airplane fly as if I were observing from a distance, equating it with the view from inside. Flying small aircraft then became a great joy. The aerobatics, mild as they were, proved to be as exciting as I had dreamed. Loops and spins were exhilarating. I wanted badly to learn more demanding maneuvers, but the little Aeronca tandem was not stressed for more. The dream of doing aerobatics "like old Speed Holman" was still unrealized.

In fact it seemed as impossible as it had a dozen years before. Flying was expensive, and the amount of time I could buy on my high-school teacher's pay was limited. Later, when I received pay for flying, the expense problem disappeared, but so did much of the fun. Flying became a job, especially when it was confined to simple point-to-point transportation. After a few years I shelved my logbook and took up more pressing matters, occasionally wondering what had happened to the old thrill of flight.

Now, twenty-some years later I realized that flying was too rare a privilege to be abandoned. The thrill must be re-experienced, but this time the flying would be strictly for fun—seat-of-the-pants flying, with a minimum of instruments and a maximum of maneuverability. I wanted a craft that would give me the freedom to hop from patch to patch, take me to all the places I wished to see, even roll inverted and turn the world upside down. The thought of such freedom brought the old excitement soaring back, and my dream of someday really flying aerobatics came alive again.

But my rekindled desire was hardly compatible with my financial condition. A plane to fill my wants would cost $20,000, and I could barely muster a tenth of that figure. I searched the flying magazines, aeronautical advertising publications and aircraft sales lists for a solution. But of the thousands of planes offered for sale, none fitted both my need and ability to pay. While reading the ads, I had noticed a number of homebuilt aircraft for sale. I wasn't interested in purchasing one, but the idea of building my own plane surfaced as a possible solution.

Several years earlier I had visited a man who was building an airplane in his garage. He had been at it for three years and expected to finish in three more. I had dismissed any thought of undertaking such a long-term project, but now my thinking was different, and Bill Bourret's plane deserved a closer look.

Bill was a big happy sort, tickled to show the intricacies of his plane and describe the problems encountered in its construction. His three-place Stits Playmate was sitting on its tricycle landing gear awaiting construction of the folding wings. His workmanship was outstanding, and I doubted that I could possibly equal its quality on a similar project in a shorter time. But Bill claimed that some home builders had finished projects in two or three years, and he dug out a dozen copies of *Sport Aviation* that carried stories proving the point. He loaded me up with reading material and ruined my sleep for a week.

Plans for more than 100 aircraft were available to the home builder, but one aircraft stood out. Its elliptical wings and gently curved fuselage enchanted my eye and crowded my imagination.

It was called the Stolp Adams Starduster, all nineteen feet of it. It was small for maneuverability, single place so I would never be tempted to fly passengers for hire, fully aerobatic to fulfill my long held dream and an open-cockpit biplane just for the hell of it. "Starduster"—what a name for a dream-chasing machine. The decision was made; I had found my new windmill. A windmill I could tilt at with great enthusiasm.

The passions of building and flying would both be satisfied.

14

It would be a long, painful endeavor, but what challenge was ever easy? My wife, Jay understood my desire to fulfill an old dream and, in the doing, spice up a life that had lost some of its excitement. She heartily endorsed the plan. I suspect that she may have had a weakness for flying machines ever since I courted her by airplane.

Time would be no real problem. My job at the local college would let me spend all my vacations, including the three-month summer layoff, on the construction. However, my salary would be no great help to the new project, and Jay and I figured our finances could handle the strain only if we put off buying a new car for a few years. I calculated that the plane would cost a bit more than $3,000. We could scrape up about $1,500 and could scrounge perhaps $500 a year for the three or so years of construction. Of course I wouldn't be doing much traveling, hunting or fishing, for the money formerly spent on those pleasures would now have to go toward the plane. It was an appropriate moment for Jay to undertake a little horse-trading. I could build my plane if she could have a three-speed bicycle, and when the plane was done, my next project would have to be the construction of her often-promised and ever-postponed greenhouse.

The next morning I ordered a set of plans for $25.00 and set out, checkbook in hand, in search of a suitable engine. There were five hangars spaced along the half-mile flight line at the Natrona County International Airport, and in one of them I found exactly what I wanted: a 125 h.p. Lycoming 0-290-D. Stacked next to the engine was a pile of parts: landing gear, a bent fuselage, a mangled propeller and a set of uncovered wings. The owners had hoped to rebuild the aircraft, but the cost of labor added up to more than the restored aircraft was worth. I offered $800.00 for the works. The owners countered with $900.00, and we settled for the midpoint.

It took a week to sort the wreck into two stacks. The one containing the engine, wheels and instruments represented those items that would become a part of the new plane. The other stack was salvage and junk. The junk went to the junkyard in exchange for a five-dollar bill that was quickly converted to a sheet of 4 x 8 particle board which would become the workbench for jigging the steel tubing fuselage. An air parts trader in Denver named Duff took the wings and some landing-gear parts in trade for a carburetor heat box, heel brakes, air filter, an old rusted throttle quadrant and nearly a hundred dollars in cash. This money was in turn converted into an assortment of steel tubing.

When the plans arrived I set to the chore of adding up the quantities of sheet-steel, straight-grained spruce and aviation-grade plywood that I would need. After firing off three airmail orders to different supply houses that specialized in aircraft materials, I began a program of study on the twenty or so sheets of plans.

Some of the drawings were baffling, and required hours of study. I found a number of dimensional discrepancies. Most corrections to be made in the plans were obvious, but others required new sketches, perspectives and three-view drawings to determine the solution. The landing-gear detail was particularly confusing, and when I mocked up a rough model, I found that if the parts were made according to plan, there would be too little propeller clearance. So I redesigned the gear to provide the clearance I wanted. It was all rather reminiscent of the way I had once designed model aircraft.

With the fuselage pattern laid out full size on the two-foot by sixteen-foot workbench, steel tubing could be cut to length, fitted in place and tack-welded. Next, I would have to bend the fuselage sides to join at the tail, while keeping them parallel in the forward section. Meanwhile, a multitude of cross members would have to be fitted and tack-welded in place.

The first of a number of problems became painfully obvious when I examined my initial attempts to weld steel tubing. The welds were patchy and lacked penetration, the result of too little heat. But whenever I got the metal hot enough, I would burn a hole right through the tubing wall, to the accompaniment of a ghastly whistling howl as the flame entered the tube. I learned to hate that sound. Luckily my mistakes were made on small pieces of spare tubing, but I did not dare tackle the final welds on the fuselage until I somehow mastered the art of welding.

I sought the advice of experts. Much help was offered and accepted, but still my welds were shamefully lumpy. At first I blamed the torch, then the regulators and finally the goggles. It seemed to me that goggles worn over bifocal glasses were an unsatisfactory combination, for the glasses steamed over at each

16

critical moment. In desperation I took the welding goggles to the local optometrist and asked that correcting lenses be ground so that I might see without glasses.

I became an instant expert. The puddle of molten metal, clearly visible for the first time, seemed to crawl along under perfect control, growing with the addition of welding rod, melting ahead, solidifying behind, just as the book said it should. For practice, I welded up every broken item I could find: a metal chair, the boat trailer, the truck bumper, the ironing board, then finally the fuselage of my airplane.

But I had developed a bad habit. After completing a weld, I would unconsciously point the torch away while I studied the weld. The smell of something burning would be the first indication that I had set a fire behind me. The curtains, the broom handle and corners of two sheets of plans all went up in flames. So a new piece of equipment had to be added—a fire extinguisher!

It took ten weeks to build the fuselage, and another month to bend and weld the tail surfaces. A few weeks later, the specially lengthened landing gear was finished and bolted in place. I then wrestled the elastic loops called shock-cords into position. Each gear could now pivot outward, the cord stretching, acting as a shock absorber. Upside down, the fuselage and landing gear looked like a spavined dinosaur. Right side up, it looked beautiful. I climbed into the space that would eventually become the cockpit and let my imagination take over. If a scarf had been handy I could have whipped it about my neck. On the third "Vroom, Vroom," my wife opened the garage door to check the new sound. She caught me jazzing the imaginary throttle of an imaginary engine on a wingless plane. I blushed; she grinned.

I soon learned that most people are unable to comprehend why anyone would want to build his own airplane. And not understanding, they are quick to condemn the effort as foolish. "Boy, you won't catch me riding in it," or "I believe in keeping one foot on the ground." One unbeliever went so far as to ask if he could take an insurance policy on my life. But fortunately my closest friends were inclined to be understanding, and I found that fellow pilots were at once encouraging and actually envious. My colleagues at the small college where I teach quickly split into two groups: those who figured I could build and fly the plane, and those who knew I would never fly it because they sure as hell wouldn't.

As the airplane progressed, I kept discovering new material needs, and the projected total cost of the aircraft began to rise menacingly above the original $3,000 estimate. Meantime, I busily went on sending off orders for seat belts, shoulder harness, windshield, fiberglass turtleback, cowl, hundreds of bolts, machine screws and tubing for the engine mount.

The engine mount is considered a most critical item in a small aircraft. This network of steel tubing that connects the engine to the airframe is subject to extreme vibration and therefore to subsequent cracking due to metal fatigue. Only welds of the highest quality can be allowed. My welding had gotten about as good as it was ever going to get by the time the fuselage and gear were finished. It was still short of perfection, but to delay construction of the engine mount would bring no improvement. So with an elaborate jig attached to the front of the fuselage, I carefully fitted the chrome molybdenum tubing in place, cleaning the tubing inside and out to prevent weld contamination. The jig was built intentionally "crooked" to allow the engine to point two degrees to the right and down a degree and a half. The right thrust was to help counteract the effect of torque—the tendency of a plane to turn to the left when the propeller turns to the right; the down thrust was to help minimize any nose-up tendency when the throttle was opened wide.

When all members of the engine mount had been tack-welded in place, I removed the whole mount from the jig and put it on the bench, where I set about the final welding. When I finished welding each cluster, I thoroughly heated it and immediately immersed it in a box of dry lime, which acted as an insulator, permitting slow cooling of the weld and thus prevented embrittlement. It was a laborious process, but it went well.

Then, on the final weld, I ruined the entire mount. The nearly completed mount was in the vise, and I was welding on a last "finger plate," or reinforcing layer of sheet metal, when the tubing bent sharply as the weight of the mount took advantage of heat-softened metal. I was sick—four days and ten bucks' worth of tubing wasted. I could repair the mount, but to install a repaired part on a brand-new aircraft was intolerable. There was

18

nothing for it: I scrapped the mount and ordered more tubing.

The most frustrating thing about building an airplane is the endless duplication and repetition. Hardly anything comes out right on the first try. Either you find a flaw in the workmanship, or you discover an error in the plans, or a part doesn't fit right. Whenever you think that improvement could be made by doing something over, then the work you've already done begins to look less and less satisfactory. You worry over its reliability until you finally make the improvement, no matter how onerous the job may be, because the prospect of test flying an aircraft with known flaws becomes less acceptable as the time for testing approaches. Fear keeps the airplane builder honest.

Summer vacation had arrived and the tubing for the second engine mount had not. Rather than sit and wait, I loaded the engine into the pickup and headed for Park Rapids, Minnesota, and the welcome assistance of an old friend.

Bill Riedesel was a friend by choice, a onetime boss by necessity and a cousin by chance. From 1944 to 1955, Bill, who operated the Park Rapids Municipal Airport, hired me during the summers as a mechanic's helper and part-time pilot. We worked well together, thinking ahead to each other's needs, generally offering or accepting needed tools or parts without question or request. Occasionally the mechanical work was interrupted by the opportunity to fly cross-country. On nonpassenger flights, I was permitted to build time for my commercial license. It was a good life, full of excitement and new experience.

When Bill learned that I planned to build my own plane, he promptly offered to supervise the work on the engine, whether it be a partial or major overhaul. The extent of required work could only be determined as the engine was disassembled. As it turned out, the engine was full of surprises!

The little Lycoming had figured in at least three serious accidents. The crankshaft had been replaced and the entire engine had been overhauled several times. The most disagreeable surprise, however, came when we looked behind the accessory case at the rear of the main housing: A whole chunk of the casing had been broken out, probably by some small engine part that had come loose. Also, two of the four bolts holding the gear wheel to the back of the camshaft were missing, the safety washers never having been bent alongside the bolts to prevent their loosening. We found part of one bolt in the oil screen. The other had either been completely chewed up or thrown out through the hole in the accessory case.

After we had completely disassembled the engine, we cleaned and inspected all the moving parts and shipped them off to Minneapolis for magnafluxing, a surefire test for small cracks invisible to the naked eye. Since there was now time to kill while waiting for replacement parts, I flew and fished and swapped stories with Bill Riedesel.

They call it hangar flying whenever two or more pilots talk shop. Such conversations are usually marked by noisy sound effects and much arm waving; truth and accuracy are seldom encountered.

"Remember the time that student pilot ran into bad weather?"

"Yup—he was taught to make a one-eighty, but the weather was so bad he made two of them just to be sure!"

"How about the time I saved the cub that was headed for the junk pile?"

Inevitably Bill claimed he had no clear recollection of the incident. It was an unwritten law that if one of us ever "greased in" an airplane—especially a crippled airplane—to a perfect landing, the other would never admit to having noticed.

The junk-pile incident began when a customer brought in a J-3 Cub with the complaint that the engine had developed a bad tendency to quit. The owner swore that he hadn't been using car gas, our first diagnosis. We checked the Cub over, and Bill gave it a test flight. The wind was brisk, and the Cub leaped off the ground quickly. The engine hummed smoothly as Bill climbed to 800 or 900 feet. Then there was a sudden silence. I watched Bill glide in to a flawless three-point dead stick landing. As we pushed the plane back to the hangar to work on the engine, Bill asked if I had seen the landing.

"Gosh, Bill, I missed it—what happened—you didn't bend anything, I hope."

After a time we were sure we had found the trouble: The

primer had been left in the unlocked position, a common cause for engine failure. With the problem corrected, I suggested that it was my turn to fly the plane. The wind had come up a bit and I looked forward to a quick take-off.

"Bet I can get her off in a hundred feet."

Bill studied the wind, looked at my skinny 120-pound frame and took me up on the bet—the loser to buy pop and peanuts all around. We paced off 100 feet (Bill now claims it was more like 100 yards) along the ramp that was facing into the wind, argued a bit over the distance and marked the spot with an old hunk of two by four. When Bill swung the prop, the engine caught immediately. I checked the magnetos and other vital signs, taxied to the starting point and ran the engine to full throttle with the brakes locked. The tail rose and I let her go. The Cub rolled rapidly toward the two by four. Twenty feet short of the mark, I asked the plane to fly with a firm pull on the stick. She was ready, and with the help of a gust of wind we cleared the board by a foot or two. I settled the Cub into a steep climb, nose pointing 30 degrees above the horizon. Just as I crossed the east-west runway, the engine quit!

My God, it was quiet! My 45 mph airspeed dribbled to 30. I popped the stick forward in self-defense, trying to regain flying speed. I tried to turn in line with the runway, but my meager hundred feet of altitude faded rapidly, forcing me to straighten and prepare to land. It was apparent that the little Cub was going to quit flying right in the middle of the airport bone pile, the junkyard of airplane parts. It would be handy anyway. The wreckage would be well placed.

My racing mind suddenly picked up on an incident I remembered from my pre-solo days. An instructor had once ruined a would-be perfect landing by shoving the stick hard forward just as the plane was about to touch. The landing gear had flexed and bouced the trainer 20 feet in the air.

A dozen feet short of the junk pile and about a foot off the ground, I jammed the stick forward. The wheels hit the ground, the landing gear spread and rebounded. The plane bounced wildly and we sailed up and over the junk pile and floated to a safe landing on an intersecting runway. Since no one showed up to offer congratulations, let alone help push the plane, I chocked the wheels with pieces of junk and cranked away until the engine fired, then taxied to the hangar, parked and walked into the office. Bill was just hanging up the phone.

"That was the owner of the Cub. Says he loaned it to a friend and the friend put some car gas in it. Ethyl, in fact— explains a lot doesn't it? Everything go all right?"

Within a week, the required engine parts arrived. The power plant went together nicely, but the parts for the engine increased the projected cost of the plane by another $500.00. I now figured the completed aircraft would cost about $3,500.00. That was higher than I had planned, but I figured that every dollar spent repairing the engine was an investment in peace of mind. I drove the long miles home, confident that the little Lycoming would be a reliable trouble-free source of power.

I hadn't been home more than a few minutes when I received an odd phone call. The operator said it was a collect call from Oklahoma and gave the name of a caller I didn't know. I was about to refuse the call when the man mentioned the word *Starduster*. I accepted immediately.

"I'm with the Federal Aviation Administration, and I'm calling about the registration number you applied for three months ago—you didn't really want that big 5-digit number, did you?"

I answered something to the effect that it was the number on the wreck I had bought.

"Well, that doesn't mean you have to use that number on your little Starduster—probably wouldn't have room for it on the fuselage anyway."

The situation was puzzling—here was a government employee calling me collect to offer advice on my plane.

"How would you like November One November Whiskey?"

"Why would I want that number?" I countered, still confused.

"It's your initials. You know, N.W. I just checked and number one for those initials is available. Of course, if you want that old number—"

"No, no! I'll take the N1NW, and thanks—sorry I'm so slow

to catch on. Guess I'd better learn the new phonetic alphabet."

I thanked him again for his help, amazed at the initiative the gentleman had taken on my behalf. There is a certain brotherhood between those who love airplanes. It surfaces quickly when a little homebuilt biplane is involved.

Enthusiasm renewed, I attacked the project with vigor, anxious to complete the plane. If the reaction of the man in Oklahoma was typical, then I was in for some real fun flying the little plane about the country.

More than a year had slipped by, and the plane was still less than half done. The fuselage was structurally complete and the engine had been mounted. The control stick was in place and connected to the elevator. But a hundred other chores remained to be done before work on the wings could start. My slow progress was due mainly to my own finicky nature, but some of the blame fell on the continuous flow of visitors.

Some of the visitors were welcome. Fellow pilots and homebuilders were often of help when an extra pair of hands was needed, but the majority of the visitors were pestiferous. Some thought they were doing me a big favor by stopping by. Invariably they would ask if I were really going to fly it, and wasn't that dangerous. I always resisted the temptation to quote Thoreau's statement about people living lives of quiet desperation, never daring to take a chance. I learned to dread the inevitable question, "Can you get it out of the garage?" That query was invariably followed by the old story of the boat in the basement.

One charming lady was very disappointed in the airplane's limited capacity.

"Aren't you going to take anyone else along?"

"Nope. Only has one seat."

"But I wanted to fly to Denver with you."

"Guess we can't do it," I answered.

"Oh yes we can," she replied, her face suddenly bright with inspiration. "We'll just make two trips!"

Space became critical in the double garage when I laid the big plywood sheets out on sawhorses in order to assemble the upper wing. The garage hadn't held a car for a year and a half, and

Jay now referred to it as the "shop." In cold weather, after her car failed to start, she pronounced *shop* with a special inflection.

The upper wing would be 19 feet long—big for a "two-car shop," but alarmingly small for an airplane. Even though I knew that a second, albeit smaller, set of wings would be added, the lifting surface seemed inadequate. Even Jay was beginning to find it difficult to believe that the craft would fly. Both our minds were put at ease a few weeks later in Boulder, Colorado.

We were visiting relatives for Christmas and had driven out to see what was happening at the local airport. As we parked, a young man appeared, pushing a tiny yellow biplane onto the ramp. His name was Clark Everest, and yes, he was going to fly the plane. I paced the wingspan—17 feet—2 feet less than the wing of my Starduster. Jay and I watched Clark go through the ritual of checking the plane inside and out. In a few minutes he climbed in and, with the help of a line hand, started the engine and taxied out. His plane, a Pitts S-1A, was smaller than mine in almost every respect except power. Clark's plane had 180 horses, whereas mine would have but 125—making my Starduster a much gentler creature, I was careful to point out.

Clark poured the cobs to the engine and came snorting down the runway. The little plane lifted just like a big craft, then climbed steeply, unlike any other craft, big or little. Jay was impressed and reassured, and I was anxious to get home to get back to work on the wings—they would look big enough now.

An old hand at airplane building once claimed that it took him a month to build the fuselage, a month to build the tail surfaces, another month to build the wings, then three more years to finish the airplane. I was beginning to find out what he meant.

When the wings were finished, the real work began. The upper wing had to be carefully aligned with the fuselage, the flat garage ceiling serving as a reference plane. With the wing tenuously supported by 1 x 2 scaffolding and brace wires, I set about fitting and tack-welding the cabane struts that connected the fuselage to the upper wing. I then temporarily bolted on the lower wings and carefully measured both wings for proper alignment and perpendicularity with the center line of the fuselage. The garage became a maze of wooden braces, plumb lines and level wires. Visitors were banned while I undertook the laborious process of building the interplane members, or I-struts. Shaped like a slanted capital "I", the struts keep the wings separated and properly aligned.

Flying wires at last brought complete rigidity to the whole structure. Crisscrossed between the wings, they provided the strength of a bridge truss. I could rock the entire plane by moving one wing tip up and down without a sign of flex or play. The wires were handmade of stainless steel, round and threaded at the ends, but otherwise flattened to a streamlined shape. Each of the eight wires had a breaking strength measured in thousands of pounds. The care evident in their manufacture was also evident in their price—the eight wires came to more than $300.00. The wires, a new propeller and an order sent off for a parachute now brought my projected cost to $4,600.00. An insurance dividend and the spring tax refund arrived opportunely.

The air frame was finally complete. Every wire, nut, bolt and instrument was in place. I called John Montebello of the local Federal Aviation Administration office and requested an inspection. Among other things, John was in charge of homebuilts and accident investigation—a combination I considered unfortunate.

The inspection revealed some shortcomings. The fuel line was too short and could break with vibration. Some bolts were faced the wrong way and the main bolt on the tail wheel was upside down. (The rule was that all bolts should face down or to the rear.) I explained that the tail wheel bolt wouldn't go in right side up. John picked up a wrench, removed the bolt and slipped it in from the top with no trouble at all. Two weeks before I had spent half an hour trying unsuccessfully to do the same thing. John pointed out a few other bolts that could be reversed. All his criticisms were valid, but damn it, everyone of them hurt!

John signed off the airframe, passing out compliments on the welding and wood work, but stipulating the changes in bolts and fuel line. Now the plane could be disassembled, covered with fabric, doped and decorated, then reassembled for the last time.

Two and a half years had passed during construction of the airframe. My colleagues at the college were tiring of asking about my progress. Those of a more acid nature continued to barb me with "ain't that plane done yet?" I assumed the "ain't" was intentional. One humorist posted a notice: "For Sale. Airplane parts, whole bunch, cheap. See Norm Weis." With encouragement like that, failure, or even delay, was unthinkable.

Covering an aircraft is a job dreaded by most builders, but for me it was frosting on the cake. During the years I had worked with Bill Riedesel, recovering aircraft had been my favorite job. Watching the skeletal framework take on solidity of form was satisfying. Lines that were already pleasing became planes and curves that felt good to the hand and brought joy to the eye.

The cover went on easily—first the fuselage bottom, then the two sides. After the glue was thoroughly dried, I gingerly applied a warm iron to the slack fabric, moving over the entire surface repeatedly. The Dacron lost its wrinkles and tightened smoothly, drawing straight lines between longitudinal members and curving sweetly to join turtleback to vertical tail fin.

Covering the wings would be easier; I approached the job with anticipation. Loose fabric laid out on the top wing brought to mind part of Ovid's tale of Icarus and Daedalus; The Fall of Icarus (Golding's translation):

> *A rowe of fethers one by one, beginning with the short, And overmatching still eche quill with one of longer sort. . . . Then fastened he with Flax The middle quilles, and joyned in the lowest sort with Wax . . . .* *

The ribs of the Starduster's wing were, in fact, of varied length—some short, some of a longer sort. They too lay row on row, overmatched by a layer of fabric and sewn through with cord well rubbed with wax.

The airplane builder would call the waxed cord ribstitching cord, and would consider its application a laborious necessity. Once you have covered both sides of the wings with fabric and shrunk it to proper tautness, you have to lay flat ribbons along the top and bottom of each rib. These ribbons must then be ribstitched in place. The stitchings, about an inch apart, have to be passed completely through the wing and securely knotted before

*From *The Poetry of Flight,* ed. by Selden Rodman. A Granger Index Reprint, Books for Libraries Press, Freeport, N.Y., ©1941.

the next stitch is laid. Without the stitching, the fabric could lift on the upper surface, distorting the airfoil, causing loss of lift, and eventually, loss of the entire cover.

After I had finished the stitching I put reinforcing tape on every ribstitch line, every seam and every wear point. Then, bedded in wet dope, each tape, when dry, had to be sanded and recoated several times. Once the tapes were firm and smooth, I gave the entire fabric surface numerous coats of dope (a quick-drying resilient form of lacquer), carefully sanding each coat with fine grit. Slowly the pinked edges of the reinforcing tape disappeared beneath the finish.

At last, with the garage as clean and dust-free as possible—even to water sprayed on the floor—I was ready to vacuum the fuselage, tail surfaces and wings and give them their final coat of color. Of all the color schemes my friends and I could devise, a scalloped red and white seemed to fit the plane's graceful lines most appropriately. The plane would appear white from top or side and red from below. When rolled it would flash each rotation with a change of color. With the addition of a blue slash across the fuselage, a large N1NW on each side, the required "Experimental" in two-inch letters over the cockpit, the job was done. Additional trim could be installed later, after testing had proved that no major alterations would be needed.

The start of another school year was only two weeks away, and the thought of fielding the same old questions with the same old answers gave me reason to plan the test flight before the first day of the new semester. I called John Montebello to arrange for final inspection. He could make it, but it would have to be August 25, and the semester started August 26. It would be a close race.

In the meantime I had to make fuel flow tests and determine the center of gravity of the plane. The latter was particularly important. Should the C.G. be too far to the rear, the plane would be unstable in a stall and tend to spin in a flat, nose level attitude from which it might not recover. If, on the other hand, the C.G. were too far forward, the plane would be reluctant to stall, would tend to porpoise and be difficult, even dangerous, to handle at lower speeds. Since the plans gave no clue as to the location of the center of gravity, I called Lou Stolp, the designer, and asked for pertinent data.

With bathroom scales borrowed from four neighbors, and the help of a few flying-type friends, the plane was rolled into position for weighing. We rested each front wheel on a cross pad connecting the tops of two scales and sat the tail wheel on a single scale raised on a platform high enough to achieve level flight position. With a little algebraic manipulation, we then established the location of the C.G. It turned out to be right where Lou and I thought it belonged.

John Montebello couldn't find anything wrong during final inspection. He even grinned a bit when he saw the tag that read "No it won't" hanging from the one bolt installed upside down. John liked the way the plane had turned out. He laid on the compliments, then twisted the good words into a safety lesson. "You be darned careful now. We don't want anything to happen to this nice little airplane, do we?" After the papers were signed, we stood and talked about the procedures and hazards of test flying a new aircraft. If it hadn't been so late in the afternoon, I would have asked him to help escort the plane to the airport for an immediate test flight.

That evening I rolled the little plane out of the garage, backing and filling to clear the 16-foot door, then positioned it on the driveway and tied it down with three stout ropes.

A little over three years of spare time and every bit of spare money I could round up sat there on the driveway. What had started out to be a $3,000.00 plane had escalated to $5,800.00, requiring a bit of cooperation from the local bank. I could have shaved perhaps a thousand or so from the total, but it would have meant going second class on important items. Now that the test flight was only hours away, I was glad that I had chosen the best materials. I went to bed confident that the aircraft was sound.

But sleep was impossible. I reviewed the last months, wondering if I had prepared myself as well as I had prepared the plane. It had taken two and a half hours of dual instruction in a Piper Cherokee 140 to bring my old skills up to the level required to pass a flight review. Four additional hours of dual in a two-place Luscombe had brought my rudder coordination back to an acceptable degree of sharpness. Luscombes are naturally nasty on the rudder, probably due to the inordinately forward position of the main landing gear. Pilots of such aircraft have to be continually on their toes—literally on their toes. Quick, short anticipatory jabs with the feet are needed in order to steer a straight course down the runway.

From midnight to 3 A.M. I flew airplanes, crashed airplanes, repaired airplanes, then flew and crashed them again. If I forced my mind away from the prospect of flight testing, a plan view of the elevator control system would immediately stretch across my closed eyes and I would inventory every nut and bolt. Finally I gave up, dressed, brewed coffee and stepped into the warm August night. I sat on the stoop and sipped from the cup, admiring the moonlight on the Starduster's wings, feeling a strange mixture of fear and anticipation.

Four hours later, the test flight behind me, still glowing with the pride of accomplishment, I confronted my colleagues at the college, waiting, just waiting for someone to ask, "How's the work on the plane coming?"

The few close friends I confided in had spread the word. Everyone seemed to know about the test flight. It was frustrating. Finally one instructor, a very predictable type, made my day by asking, "Say, did you ever finish that plane you were working on?"

And I replied with great satisfaction, "Why yes, as a matter of fact I took it up for a spin just this morning."

3/Testing

The aircraft logbook held one lonely entry:

> *Date: 8-26-75*
> *Hours: .4*
> *Pilot: N. Weis*
> *Remarks: First test, nose heavy, poor radio reception.*

The nose-heavy condition was serious. I had made a bad mistake in determining the proper location of the center of gravity. A double check on the weight and balance calculations revealed no mathematical error. The C.G. was precisely 4.6 inches ahead of the leading edge of the lower wing, right where it should have been according to the last phone conversation with Lou Stolp, the designer.

But when I reviewed the notes of earlier calls and found a second, more rearward set of center of gravity figures, it became obvious that Lou Stolp and I had discussed two different aircraft.

Lou had designed a two-place version of the Starduster at a later date, and since I failed to identify my plane on the last phone call, he naturally assumed I was building his most recent design.

The C.G. of my aircraft should have been at the leading edge of the lower wing, nearly five inches behind its present location.

The solution was obvious: move the C.G. to the rear by removing weight up front or adding it to the tail. Calculations showed that the addition of a 20-pound battery in the tail section would not suffice because I would have to add a generator up front to complete the electrical system. Another alternative would be to remove the heavy starter from the front. That would mean that the engine would always have to be hand-cranked, but there was an advantage: Leaving out the starter, generator, and battery would save more than fifty pounds and result in increased performance.

It was late afternoon and the wind was calm when I rolled the plane out of the hangar for its second flight. There was no crowd of curious on hand. Just one friend stood by as I climbed into the cockpit—and again ran the stick up my pant leg. I quickly drafted my friend to crank the prop.

While the engine warmed, I reviewed the changes I had made in the plane and mentally prepared myself for a new, perhaps unexpected feel on the controls. The starter was gone, a 4-pound chunk of lead had been bolted to the tailspring and the leading edge of the horizontal stabilizer had been lowered a bit. The new C.G. now *should* be within half an inch of the correct position.

Takeoff was the same mind-bending thrill. Tail up, accelerating, wheels off and climbing—climbing steeply. In minutes we were a mile above the ground.

Trimmed out, the little plane flew hands off—literally hands off! I flew with both arms out in the slipstream and wiggled the palms alternately up and down. I could bank it right and left with the air pressure on my hands! If I leaned forward, the plane dove gently. If I leaned back **and** pulled up my knees, she climbed. What a kitten! Flying was effortless. Think a turn to the left and before the thought could end, the path flight curved. Imagine a spiral climb and the next instant you are looking down from new heights while the wing tip draws small circles across a fading earth.

Some moves the plane seemed to do entirely by herself, and rarely did I feel that I was in complete command—that *I* moved the levers and the machine responded. *We* climbed and banked and soared. *We* topped the clouds and mottled them with our fleeting shadow. *We* moved from wingover to wingover, climbing easily to each swooping apex to stand breathless on a wing tip, then dive, level and rise to yet another weightless falling turn.

Finally, *I* retarded the throttle, and *I* kicked the rudder to point the way back to the airport. With some reluctance the Starduster obliged. *We* sliced down the invisible path and let the ground meet us with gentle contact.

Clearly, the little plane was built for aerobatics. She held promise of a thousand moves I had never dared try. Try them I would, but first the plane must be thoroughly tested, and before the testing could start, the problem with the radio had to be solved.

As a physicist, it was embarrassing for me to admit failure with a simple thing like a transmitter and receiver, but as I explained to would-be helpers, electromagnetic radiation wasn't my speciality. After trying three locations for the antenna, and half a dozen different headsets and mikes, I gave up and rewired the external circuitry. I have no idea what portion of the wiring had been faulty, but I welcomed the sudden improvement in reception without question for fear the questioning would cause a sudden return of the problem. Radios work best if the operator has faith. As we physicists know, radios can sense a suspicious mind and always react vindictively.

There were many tests to be made before the plane could be considered safe in all categories. Fuel-starvation trials headed the list. The 22-gallon fuel tank in the Starduster's nose owed its capacity in part to its deep, belly-shaped bottom, which rode only four inches above the carburetor when the plane was in level flight. In a steep climb, the tank bottom rode at an even lower level—so low that the last three or four gallons of gas could not be trusted to flow by gravity to the carburetor. A curved, hollow blast tube facing forward on the gas cap permitted air to be forced into the tank to pressurize the fuel and minimize the possibility of fuel starvation. I had installed a ball-check valve in the blast tube to prevent wholesale loss of fuel when the aircraft was inverted.

To test the adequacy of the fuel system, I climbed "normally" to 12,000 feet over the airport, then proceeded to climb as steeply as possible at full throttle. By holding the plane on the edge of a stall, the altitude and attitude could be held constant. Periodically I leveled the plane and checked the fuel gauge. With only two gallons remaining, the engine continued to run flawlessly. I decided to try a steeper angle of climb, but a dive to speed would be required. I hadn't mentioned such plans to the tower, so I called and asked permission. They answered with a question. "What is your present altitude?"

"Eleven thousand five hundred."

"Our control zone tops out at twelve thousand feet."

"Okay, I'll climb to thirteen and terminate above twelve."

Diving sharply from 13,000 feet the speed increased rapidly. The air-speed needle wound to the right like a clock gone crazy. At 150 I eased back on the stick and held on as the nose passed horizontal and reached steeply upward. I held the angle until the speed faded. The blast tube had done its job: The engine had run smoothly with no sign of fuel shortage. The accelerometer, or g meter, read a positive two and a half, which meant that my frame and the Starduster's airframe had felt a load 2½ times our normal weight. My body had exerted a force of 400 pounds against the seat, and the wings had supported nearly 3,000 pounds. The plane was designed to take up to 10 g's, but I suspected that my body was somewhat less tolerant.

I dove again, planning a 3-g pull up. When the speed reached 160, I gave the stick a firm pull. My innards sagged and the seat compressed. My head felt heavy, then suddenly light as the plane climbed almost vertically. The g meter read an even 4 g's. The engine had operated smoothly throughout. I decided there was no problem with the fuel system and directed my attention to the establishment of a "do not exceed speed" and a maximum personal g tolerance.

There was a possibility that something might go wrong as dive speeds were increased. The first sign of trouble would probably show up in the form of vibration, and the most likely spot would be the ailerons. If an aileron began to vibrate I would have little time to back off on the speed before the aileron would break up. If the aileron went, chances were the wings would go shortly after. I disconnected the radio plugs and stuffed them down my shirt front, tightened the chute straps, unhooked my second seat belt and rehearsed the procedure for bailing out. The special pains I had taken during the construction of the cockpit now paid great dividends in peace of mind. I had moved the instrument panel forward two inches and shifted the top of the backrest rearward three inches. As a result, I could exit the plane in an emergency by placing my feet flat on the floor, and after releasing the single lever on the seat belt and shoulder harness, catapult myself straight up and out. Most biplanes required a straight-legged exit by brute force of the arms on either the cockpit coaming sides or wing-mounted hand grips. Once out of the aircraft, there would be no counting, simply a clawing search for the D ring, and that longest of waits for the canopy to deploy.

With power on this time, I dove until the speed reached 165, then pulled back firmly on the stick. My jaw sagged as the g forces set in. I could feel the viscera crowd lower in the body cavity. The meter read 5½. I gave the wings a quick visual check as the plane zoomed back to 13,000 feet, realizing I had neglected to watch the ailerons for flutter. I let the speed build to 170 on the next dive and held it there for a quick check on the ailerons, then pulled up abruptly—5 g's again. I wondered about the effects of heavy g forces as I regained altitude. Test pilots had been known to suffer from severe hemorrhoids—even complete rectal inversion. I decided to tighten up the belly and yell bloody murder on the next pull up. Down again—175—right aileron okay—left aileron okay. I yelled as the g's grew and then faded. The meter read 6. I noticed that I had unconsciously been holding down the mike switch on the stick. If the mike jack had been plugged in, I would have broken the eardrums of everyone in the tower.

The speed climbed to 178 on the next dive. The ailerons showed no sign of vibration. I gave the stick a brutal pull and yelled my way through a record 6½ g's, then climbed to bleed off the airspeed. The engine coughed, sputtered, then came back to life as I headed down at reduced throttle, conserving the little gas remaining. I turned in tight circles, remaining over the airport, reconnecting earphones and mike jacks, and loosening chute straps that suddenly felt uncomfortably tight. The landing was uneventful.

Once in the hangar, I removed all the inspection plates in order to give the plane a thorough going over. Nothing had moved or loosened. The flying wires still strummed middle C, and the wings could be rocked from the tip without a sign of flex. A bystander observing the seemingly rough treatment given the plane asked the reason for all the wiggling and shaking. I explained how g forces had put a heavy strain on the plane making thorough inspection necessary. He looked at the accelerometer, still reading 6½ g's, then straightened up and uttered a classic "Boy, if it's that hard on the plane, think what it does to your asteroids!"

Spinning an airplane is simple. In a Piper Cub or an old Aeronca Champ, the maneuver can even be enjoyable, but spinning the Starduster was something else. I had spent several evenings studying and memorizing the NASA (National Aeronautics and Space Administration) spin-recovery techniques. NASA recommended full abrupt, opposite rudder, followed by an equally abrupt forward movement with the stick, in case neutralization of the controls (—that is, centering the stick and bringing the rudder pedals even with one another) failed to break the plane's spin. Actually, neutralization of the controls was a procedure to be used only in testing. If you could recover within one turn, the plane could be considered normal. (In protracted spins, neutralization recovery might require two revolutions.) But in no circumstances were you supposed to use power or ailerons, for the application of either could cause the nose to rise, locking the plane into the dreaded flat spin. Since location of the C.G. too far to the rear could have the same result, the C.G. problems I had already experienced contributed little to my peace of mind. If the spin went flat, I promised myself two tries at the NASA recovery before bailing out.

The plane entered the first spin nicely. With the controls immediately neutralized, the spin terminated in the expected half-turn. After one full turn, recovery was equally easy. But the two-turn spin brought my education to a new level. The Starduster had a two-stage entry: nice and easy on the first turn, then rapid as hell on the second. In a panic, I used the full emergency procedure, shoving in all the opposite rudder and forward stick I could find. To cope with spinning at that frightening rate—nearly one turn per second—by simply neutralizing the controls required more cool than I could muster.

I climbed back to 13,000 and had a little conference with myself. I didn't really want to find out what surprise the plane might have in store during the third and fourth turns, but if I chickened out now, all my hopes of doing aerobatics would have to be abandoned. I would never know the thrill of performing "just like Speed Holman."

So I pulled on the carburetor heat, slowed to a stall, kicked hard right rudder and held full back stick, scared but determined to try for three turns. The plane again spun slowly on the first turn then whipped violently into the second. But mercifully the rate of rotation held constant for turn number 3. My recovery, again with frantic full opposite controls, was accomplished in the expected half-turn. Greatly relieved, I climbed back and tried three turns to the left, then four turns right and four turns left.

My cool was returning. I tried several more four-turn spins, determined now to recover with controls neutralized instead of jammed full opposite. But it was impossible. I tried counting out loud—"1—2—3—NEUTRALIZE!" but each time adrenaline rose and I shoved in full opposite controls. I called it quits at 5 turns left and 5 right with full opposite recovery, then headed for the airport and solid ground. After landing, I sat for a few moments in the Starduster's now-silent cockpit, vowing to myself that someday, somehow, I'd find the courage that had failed me today.

On several occasions during the past couple of days the tower operator had asked me if I cared to make a low approach. Each time I had refused because I did not know what a low approach was, and hated to broadcast my ignorance by asking. A fellow pilot later explained that it was simply a low-level pass. If that was the case, I could certainly oblige. Apparently they wanted an old-fashioned buzz job, and that was something I understood.

On my next takeoff I keyed the mike and asked if they still wanted me to make a low approach. The man in the tower gave an affirmative, and I explained that I would climb to 400 feet, make a

180 and dive down to pass between the tower and the runway at eye level.

"Affirmative on your plan."

The plane was twenty feet off the ground, traveling at 160 mph, as the tower passed by my rocking wings.

"Very pretty, Starduster Whiskey, now look out for the Citabria on final for runway two-five."

"I have him—I'll make a climbing turn out."

Still at full throttle, I bent the plane around the end hangar, climbing steeply, feeling a new camaraderie with the men in the tower. Later, one of them told me that my "low approach" was a bit unusual, and that I really should have avoided the steep turn, and maybe should have cleared that hangar by a few more feet, but he grinned as he said it.

About a mile from my home in the suburbs, a long flat hayfield offered a tempting opportunity for a convenient "back-yard" landing. I had eyed it carefully each time I flew out on the now almost routine test flights. An off the airport landing would be a break in the testing program. Mel Loose, who grew several crops of hay on the irrigated land each season, was agreeable to letting me land on the field between cuttings, pointing out that the small irrigation dikes fortunately ran lengthwise along the 2,100-foot strip. We had toured the field by car, running the length several times at 50 mph to check for bumps.

The next day I informed the tower of my plans, since the field was within their control zone, and then proceeded to "drag" the field, flying slowly along the ground, noting trees along the edge and the telephone lines at the north end. On the second pass I rolled the Starduster's wheels 100 yards or so, then took off and went around again. My antics had drawn a small crowd. Mel drove out to watch, and several cars stopped on the road. Later I found out one of them was an FAA official.

On the third pass I rolled the wheels on at the south end, slowed to a stop midway in the field and waited for Mel to drive alongside in his truck. We chatted for a while about how smooth the field was and how the irrigation dikes were of no real hazard. I told Mel that I would taxi to the telephone lines, then turn and take off downwind to the south. Being a pilot himself, he agreed it was the best choice. I asked if he wanted to drive alongside on takeoff and compare speeds. He agreed and I taxied to the north end, Mel following in the truck.

The people on the road, including the man from the FAA, saw a different picture. They saw an irate rancher drive out and demand the removal of the plane from his land. Then they saw the rancher chase the plane to the north end, where the plane evaded the truck with a sharp turn, and then—believe it or not—the rancher, madder than hell by now, chased that guy in the plane right off his land!

On takeoff it must have looked that way, since the Starduster immediately left Mel behind. I held the plane down a bit longer than needed, and in the process drifted over one of the irrigation dikes. The prop chewed away at the earth, throwing up a cloud of dust that added a bit of drama to the occasion.

A few days later, after inspecting the prop for damage, I had a chance to put the worried officials at ease, explaining that I had permission to land on the "Mel Loose Hayfield International Airport" at any time, provided the irrigation water was turned off and the crop was short.

The next phase of my testing program would also involve g tests, but this time they would be eye-popping negative g's. I decided to break in slowly, starting with zero g's.

The weightlessness of zero gravity is delightful. Most youngsters love it the first time they are tossed in the air. Divers and trampolinists enjoy it briefly as they round out their trajectories. In an airplane the effects of zero g can be extended to 10 or 12 seconds if the controls are handled properly. The speed must be increased with a gentle dive, then the plane put in a climb and carefully rounded out with forward pressure on the stick. If this is done correctly, the plane can be flown across the crown of this vertical curve in a perfectly weightless condition. A pen placed on the dash can be "lifted" a few inches and floated at eye level, then gently replaced as positive g's are returned.

Years earlier I had sometimes fought boredom on cross-country trips by playing a little game with my cap. Placed on the dash, upside down and bill facing to the rear, it could be lifted with careful application of forward stick. Once it was above the dash, by advancing the throttle I could fly my head, airplane and all, forward under the cap, and by touching the bill to my forehead,

I could tip the cap onto the top of my head. Admittedly, sometimes I would prolong the maneuver unduly and the plane would end up in a steep heart-stopping dive.

But flying at zero g's is not all fun and games. Dirt and grit tend to rise from hiding places in the floorboards, inevitably finding their way into eyes, nose and mouth. Larger objects float from the floor to skylight. At various times I have plucked long-lost items from midair—pens, sunglasses, a pocketknife and, on one memorable occasion, eighty-five cents in change.

The situation changes when you shift from zero g to a negative two. Your eyeballs rise to the top of your head and are crowded by rising cheeks that threaten to close your eyelids from the bottom. Your entire body strains against the seat belt and shoulder harness, and in an open cockpit, the threat of being unseated and consequently deplaned is all too real. It would be even worse in the Starduster because the engine would quit instantly when the plane went negative. The prop would continue to windmill, but the sudden loss of noise and thrust was bound to be upsetting. On top of that, some of the gasoline rising to the top of the tank would undoubtedly spurt out of the blast tube before the ball check valve could seat. At least half a cup of gas would wash over the windshield and quickly evaporate, leaving a short-lived trail of moisture condensed from the sudden cooling.

Uncomfortable or otherwise, the plane had to be tested negative. I climbed, and at 110 mph "pushed over" until the g meter read a minus 3½. That was well past my personal preference. Every discomfort I had foreseen was realized—in spades. I called it quits and decided quite unprofessionally that any further tests in that direction would have to arrive by accident.

The general unpleasantness of negative g's made the prospect of trying some maneuvers, even spins, enjoyable by contrast. I decided that I would try one more time to recover from a 4-turn spin with simple neutralization. Once again shouting at myself, "1—2—3—Neutralize," I managed this time to stop control movement at neutral position. To my horror the spin went on: 5, 6 and finally—finally the plane straightened. I had done it—barely—but I was quite shaken. I wondered how much worse an inverted spin would be, and in particular, how much slower the recovery might be. The thought raised my stomach to my throat.

If anyone had told me then that within a year I would be spinning the plane inverted, I would most certainly have said he was crazy.

The structural tests were now completed. I entered an endorsement in the aircraft logbook:

> *At 25.1 hours total time this aircraft is considered to be free of adverse characteristics and capable of handling aerobatic maneuvers.*
>
> *and I signed it!*

I was soon to discover that a good test report does not make the plane immune to trouble. A week later, while I was sightseeing over the rugged canyon-cut, southern foot of the Big Horn Mountains, the engine began stuttering. I headed east, looking for flat ground and frantically checking the fuel level and engine instruments. Everything appeared normal, but the engine continued to hiccup every few seconds. Twenty worrisome minutes later I entered the airport control zone on a high pattern, allowing for possible engine failure, then slipped sharply to a landing.

The carburetor was wet with gasoline and still dripping. Obviously something was holding the float valve open. That meant the cowling, air-box, assorted engine controls and the carburetor itself had to be removed to get at the trouble. Finally the culprit was found—a 2-inch dog hair lodged alongside the float valve. In the sediment bowl I found two more hairs waiting their opportunity to add a little excitement to the next excursion over the mountains. I dismantled and purged the fuel system from tank to firewall, but found no further dog hairs. I suppose the hair had found its way into the tank when I blew it dry with a vacuum cleaner after pressure testing the tank with water. I should simply have let nature take its course and let the water flush out with the first fill of gasoline. Perfectionism tends to compound the simple.

I took off the next day with the power plant again running smoothly. Twenty miles out, the engine suddenly took on a new, louder sound. I thought my ears had simply popped, but that easy explanation evaporated when the cockpit began heating up. I dropped quickly to fifty feet, looking for a landing site, at the same time feeling the metal surfaces by my right and left legs. The right side was hot—too hot to keep my hand in firm contact.

Probably an exhaust stack had broken. If so, the plane was in immediate danger of catching fire and there would be no time to find a landing place. Flying low was the worst thing I could do. With throttle wide open, I climbed back to a height that would permit use of the parachute. I slowed down and punched in some right rudder, hoping the resulting slip might direct the excess heat overboard through the right cowl opening, away from the combustible fabric. The temperature of the panel by my right leg stabilized, but the ugly smell of burning paint began to drift through the cockpit.

Traffic was heavy at the airport. Landing in turn would take time. I thought about declaring an emergency, considered the possible postmortem paperwork and opted for an extended base in number-5 position, as requested by the tower.

The stack had indeed broken off, and the metal flank behind the firewall was scorched brown. I considered the needed repair to the exhaust stack and the paint job, recalling a dozen other improvements I wanted to make—stiffer trim springs, gear-leg covers, wheel pants, an oil-breather extension, wing fairings and an oil cooler to bring down the engine oil temperature. Also, since cold weather was setting in and flying would become uncomfortably chilly, I decided to add a cockpit heater to my list of changes.

A few days later, with the exhaust stack temporarily repaired, I landed the plane at Mel's "Hayfield International" and taxied down the ranch road to the outskirts of the housing development where I live. A raft of kids was on hand to push the plane the remaining few blocks. The little sweetheart was home again; a bit tired and worn from testing, but just as pretty as she had been three months before when she had stood in that same spot, bathed in moonlight.

Jay stood beside me, and we viewed the little Starduster with matching pride. Her delight in the little plane continually surprised me. At the moment the name for the plane became obvious: "Second Sweetheart." Sweetheart because she was, and "Second Sweetheart" to let Jay know she still held top priority.

4/Airshow Anyone?

It was good to have the plane home again. The garage became a shop once more as the Starduster's graceful wings filled its width. Again it became a joy to open the doorway connecting house to garage and be confronted with the promise of adventure. Now that the plane had proven herself in flight, anticipated delights were unmarred by doubt.

But I found that the return to mechanical work was also satisfying. Flying the plane, however exciting and challenging, lacked the feel of accomplishment that follows the creation of something of particular beauty or utility. Building and flying one's own airplane involved a unique combination of satisfactions. I could only regret that I had not discovered the combination earlier.

The winter passed easily and the little Starduster blossomed. Wheel pants and gear-leg covers gave the plane a rakish look that promised added speed. New metal wing fairings connected wing to fuselage, covering a multitude of air resisting protuberances. Wingwalks glued to each wing root offered slip-free access to the cockpit, but created frictional drag that probably negated the streamlining effect of the wing fairings.

Some changes I made, although unapparent, added greatly to the plane's performance or to my comfort. I reworked and strengthened both exhaust stacks, and fitted a sleeve on the right stack that allowed ambient air to be warmed and ducted to the front of the cockpit. Several old-time pilots scoffed at the idea of a heater in an open cockpit, explaining that the wash of air past the cockpit would pull out the warm air before it could be felt. But the experts were wrong. The heater later proved able to maintain reasonable comfort even with the outside air temperature at the freezing level.

After much consultation with the local radio repairman, I replaced the earphones in my helmet with stereo headphones rewired for monaural operation, and wired to the speaker outlet of the radio. The impedance of the new earphones perfectly matched that of the speaker circuit, so that what had formerly been marginal reception now became a threat to the eardrums. With the volume turned up, the empty helmet sounded like a P.A. system, and a hand placed in the helmet was bombarded with little puffs of air from both sides. I considered limiting the travel on the volume knob, but decided against it when a friend suggested it might offer a bit of poetic justice to a would-be thief.

I added black trim to accent the meeting of red and white along the fuselage, and on the vertical fin I painted a stylized heart crossed by old-fashioned letters that read SECOND SWEETHEART. With those letters, the plane was christened and declared complete.

The confinement of winter sparked plans for summer travel. Some provision had to be made for protecting the plane in strange territory. A snap-on cockpit cover made of coated nylon would offer shelter from rain and prying hands. Emergency tie-down anchors and generous lengths of rope were installed under the seat, along with an emergency kit containing signal mirror, flares and smoke bombs.

Warm Chinook winds brought a taste of spring in early March, melting the snow from Mel's hayfield airstrip and revealing numerous cow-pies the size of fat hubcaps. We cleared the larger specimens from the take-off patch and checked the entire length for gopher holes. Then, as a small camera-laden crew gathered the next morning, Second Sweetheart was rolled out of the garage and trundled down the road to the hayfield.

The air was crisp and frost covered the ground. The engine started easily, and I taxied down the strip, dodging the occasional frozen cow-pie. After checking the engine, I called the tower, two miles to the north, carefully holding the volume at a minimum. They answered immediately with information on wind velocity and altimeter setting. I informed them of my plan to take off and make a few passes down the hayfield for photographs, then squared the plane away and opened the throttle.

The tail rose quickly and, with the nose lowered, I plotted my course down the field, missing the largest of the remaining cow-pies. I was still dodging when the wheels met a small rise and we left the ground. In the cold dense air the climb was phenomenal. The old thrill of flight was back, stronger than ever. I succumbed immediately to the temptation and laid a wing down for a slipping, diving pass down the field, terminating with a sharp, nearly vertical pull up. Another pass, and I rolled the wheels on the ground, carefully missing the cow-pies, recalling the quip a friend made earlier about going up when the chips were down.

Photographs completed, I settled into respectable straight and level flight, and called the tower for clearance to land. On final approach, half a mile short of the runway, my pride in the little airplane surged to a peak. I keyed the mike and asked the tower if I could make a low approach. The response was distinctly cool, "Ah—Starduster Whiskey— Ah, what is the occasion?"

"Oh, I'd just like to show off the finished product. You might call it a low pass for therapeutic purposes."

There was a long pause, the operator no doubt recalling my earlier "low approach" that turned into a buzz job. "Starduster Whiskey, affirmative on that low approach—confine your path to runway two-one, maintain normal speed and follow standard pattern." They had my number—there would be no more grass-patch hi-jinks at this airport.

I flew down the runway at 120 mph, 100 feet off the ground, climbed to proper altitude and executed a very correct rectangular pattern, landed and taxied to the ramp full of rebellious thoughts. How much fun it would have been to fly by the tower at eye level, upside down, then key the mike and drawl out, "is my gear up?" But first I'd have to learn to fly upside down.

Appropriately, aerobatics was the next challenge on the agenda. Finally, more than 40 years after watching Speed Holman fly aerobatics at the Omaha Air Show, my chance to try the same moves had arrived.

For several months I had been reading various books on aerobatics. Invariably, the introduction made it clear that good instruction was the first requisite. But since my single-seat aircraft did not lend itself readily to dual instruction, I decided I'd better try to teach myself aerobatics, even if that meant doing it the hard way.

Knife-edge flight, or flying on the side, was the first new maneuver I wanted to learn. My favorite aerobatic book laid out the control movements in precise terms. I memorized them one evening and set out the next morning to try my hand. Three thousand feet above the ground, I rolled Second Sweetheart to the left until the wings stood perpendicular to the horizon. Immediately things began to happen—the nose dropped and the plane entered a steep diving turn. I recovered and flew back to altitude, mentally going over the author's instructions once again.

On the second try I applied more top rudder to keep the nose up. The plane responded properly for a moment, then began bucking about before dropping into the same steep diving turn.

I tried again, this time with an entry speed of 140 mph. Beautiful! The little Starduster flew straight away, nose slightly high, wings perpendicular to the ground. At 160 mph it was even better—she would hang on to the altitude nicely until the speed dropped to 120, then she would buck and bounce around, warning me it was time to level out before we stalled out.

Once knife-edge right and left were perfected, it was time to try inverted flight and rolls. The book claimed that it was simply a matter of holding the stick hard to the left, into knife-edge position and right on past, then easing off the rudder as the wings leveled with the horizon, upside down, of course. Once inverted, some forward stick pressure would be required to hold the nose up.

I might have succeeded on my first try if so many things hadn't happened in such rapid sequence. As the plane approached the inverted position, the usual cup of fuel spilled from the filler cap. As the gasoline spilled over the windshield, negative g's took up the slack in the seat belt. My body shifted downward out of the plane an inch or two, and the top of my head felt the hard buffet of the slip stream. Then, as expected, the engine quit, since the plane did not have an inverted fuel system. The propeller continued to windmill and the engine would restart when upright. But somehow the total effect was frightening. The adrenaline flowed, and I reacted with shameful panic, throwing in full opposite aileron, and pulling back on the stick. Using aileron was proper, but the back stick was a mistake. In seconds we were headed straight down, the engine again running, screaming to high rpm's as the speed built to 150, then 160. I yanked the throttle back and pulled out of the dive gradually. The speed built to 175 and the g meter wound past the 6 mark.

I gave the situation a bit of thought as I climbed back to altitude. Forward pressure and continued use of aileron would have let the roll continue to completion.

With the seat belts and shoulder harness tightened, I tried again. This time the spilling gasoline was no surprise. The negative g's were briefly uncomfortable, but soon lessened as the roll continued to the opposite knife-edge, then to upright position. The nose had wobbled all over the horizon, but the roll was accomplished. Now it would be simply a matter of perfecting the technique.

It took half a hundred tries to purge my system of all the wrong ways to roll an airplane. Finally, with the cause of each mistake recognized, I could roll the plane to the left without flaw, keeping the nose pointed steadily at some fixed point on the horizon. Trial and error is a hard but a sure way to learn. I suppose I might have learned faster, but I was under a double handicap—a slow learner taught by an inexperienced, often bewildered instructor.

Once accomplished and perfected, each new maneuver

adds to the feeling of freedom. It's a special feel that can never be felt by those limited to ground travel. The closest parallel that I can draw is with a young driver newly turned loose with a sports car fresh from the dealer's showroom. The acceleration is heady and the cornering ability impressive, but the new-found mobility is still only two dimensional. But now imagine a new feature—one that permits the driver to control the tilt of the road ahead. A turn to the right banks the road, and the car changes direction without tendency to skid. Rapid turns of the steering wheel create wide, perfectly banked S turns on the road that fit perfectly beneath the car's wheels. Pull back on the steering wheel and the road tilts upward and stretches into the sky. It can turn upside down if you wish, and then back to level. The road is always in place, curving and sweeping in tune with your every move. Make that road invisible, change the steering wheel to stick and rudder pedals and increase the sensitivity to the point of daring response, and you are in the cockpit of Second Sweetheart, riding the caprioles of a modern Pegasus.

A maneuver I had always wanted to learn was the hammerhead. It starts with the airplane pointed straight up; then, as the airspeed approaches zero, the nose drops sideways like a hammer strike. The plane continues rotating until it is pointed straight down, the wings all the while in the same geometric plane, like the arms of a youngster doing a cartwheel.

To fly truly straight up is difficult, and to fly precisely, vertically downward is alarming. In order to fly straight up, one must first gain a little extra speed—150 or so—then pull up firmly and look to the side. When you see the wings standing vertically, on the horizon, you are heading straight up. A glance to the opposite wing to check for equal spacing right and left will ensure a straight, nonleaning path of flight.

On my first try, my airspeed dribbled away before I could check both wings and the plane fell back down in a tail slide—a move that puts fantastic forces on the elevator and rudder. I hung on to the controls firmly as the reverse air flow tried to slap the control surfaces full travel. The stick moved back forcibly and the plane whipped quickly to the nose-down position. After an oscillation or two we were headed straight down. Good grief! Nothing was visible ahead but solid ground! The air speed needle wound rapidly to the right and had passed the 100 mark before I was able to ease back the stick.

On the next try, I went into a proper vertical climb and threw in full left rudder at the top. The plane wobbled over and headed down crooked and partially inverted. Three tries later it became evident that the right wing, traveling faster on the outside of the curve, was still giving lift. I tried mixing a little right aileron with the left rudder—better—more aileron—better yet.

Forty or so hammerheads later, the maneuver was predictable, but hardly perfected. The secret was to detect the approach of zero speed at the top of the climb and lay into the controls so quickly that the wings were half way around before all the speed was gone. Done properly, the controls at the apex of the climb were: full left rudder, full right aileron and almost full forward on the stick.

After I tied a three-foot piece of yarn to the left strut, the maneuver became a cinch. When the speed began to deteriorate, the ordinarily straight yarn would whip about. After one good whip, I knew that it was time to feed in the controls—full left rudder, stick in the right front corner—until the plane was straight down. When the yarn once more assumed a straight position, again perpendicular to the horizon, I could hold the nose on a point on the ground for a nice straight-down line.

New maneuvers seemed to start with apprehension, then move through alternate periods of pride and fright, followed eventually by confidence, and sometimes blasé overconfidence. That was the case with the hammerhead.

I began to think there was nothing to it. But there was one more way of fouling up the maneuver that I hadn't yet blundered upon. For some reason, perhaps it was simply curiosity, I fed in full control movement while still going up at about 60 mph. The sky went crazy! Completely disoriented, I watched the sky and ground trade places over the nose. Air rushed in from the side, then from behind, and the stick came alive in my hand. I fought it, but it went full travel forward and the plane whipped into a new mode. We were rotating, and all I could see was ground. Having been in broken maneuvers before where I just held on until the plane settled into something I understood, such as a dive or spin, I

48

wasn't greatly worried. However, I didn't recognize this movement. It felt like a spin, but no sky was visible—just brown ground. After three or four turns I decided I had better do something besides just wait it out. A suspicion that I was in an inverted spin quickly blossomed into fear. Luckily I had memorized the recovery from the dreaded maneuver, even rehearsed it.

Throttle back, full opposite rudder, wait a bit for the rotation to stop, now full BACK stick—point her for the ground! Ah, straight down—wait for speed—now pull out. The altimeter read 1000 feet above the ground as I leveled out. Damned fool! Next time you want to experiment, do it way up there where a parachute might do you some good!

A person can learn a lot from his mistakes. The secret is to survive the first mistake and never repeat it. Learning aerobatics is the same as learning anything else—but the penalty for failure is greater.

FAA regulations demand that aerobatics be conducted 1,500 feet above the ground, off the airways and away from populated areas. Aerobatics are defined as any abrupt change in direction, generally considered to be climbs or dives beyond 30 degrees and banks more than 60 degrees. Occasionally, turbulent air may cause one to exceed such limits—a handy excuse.

I had developed the same bad habits displayed by most pilots a few hours after solo: I was a complete and utter show-off. I never passed anyone on the ground without wagging my wings 60 degrees (or was it 90 degrees) each way. For two people I would add a rule-bending hammerhead and top off with a slipping turn down alongside to accept their accolades. Three or more spectators constituted a crowd and I pulled out the stops. At 1,500 feet over the ground I would treat the folks to loops, hammerheads, rolls and a few things I still wasn't sure of.

My particular weakness was schoolbuses. I could not pass one without swinging down at eye level, a few feet off the ground at a very legal 500 feet to the side, then putting the Sweetheart in a climbing "60-degree" banked knife-edge that rode on the brink of illegality. Occasionally I fractured the regulations badly, but always by "accident," or "due to turbulence." The latter was, of course, an act of God, and the former simply the result of something the devil made me do.

As a youngster, I had never failed to watch every airplane that passed overhead. Most aircraft traveled past without change in attitude. I could never figure out why a pilot of a machine that could go up and down and all about would ever settle for straight and level flight. Didn't he know his capabilities? Didn't he know I was down here watching and waiting? And didn't he know that thousands of other kids were looking up, aching to see the plane do what it was built to do, a roll, or a loop or at least a dip of the wing?

On one memorable occasion a passing plane suddenly dove, then looped—and looped again. I ran the two miles to the airport and found that the plane had just taken off. The mechanics told me all about it—how it had almost 100 horsepower, olio struts and could do almost any stunt, even spins! Since that time I took each sedate passage of an aircraft as a personal affront. I might forgive airline pilots and even the pilots of chartered aircraft, but for the pilot of an aerobatic aircraft to pass over straight and level is an insult to every envious youngster below. That's why I perform for every schoolbus I see.

The little biplane had assumed several personalities with names to match. Quite naturally she was the "Sweetheart" when she was delightful, but she became "Duster Whiskey" when bestial. Officially, she was "Starduster N1NW," but on the radio her name was "Starduster One November Whiskey." After the first call, the name is generally shortened to "November Whiskey" by the tower, but I always acknowledged the transmissions with "Duster Whiskey" to keep the operators on their toes. Occasionally a controller would counter with "Dusty Whiskers."

"Second Sweetheart" was not a part of the registration number and therefore not permitted in the communications, although I often would have preferred to call her that—particularly after a satisfying session of aerobatics. She was especially deserving of the name when she forgave the mistakes made during a sloppy landing caused by a fuzzy brain in a head still swimming from snaps and rolls.

There are four basic types of rolls one can do in an aircraft. Besides the snap rolls and slow rolls, there are the barrel rolls and falling aileron rolls. The aileron rolls are the easiest and can be accomplished in most any aircraft. The plane is aimed upward at about 30 degrees, stabilized on a straight climbing line, then the stick is pushed full travel to the side. No forward or back pressure is used. The plane rolls and falls along a curve ending up in level flight as the wings again reach the horizontal. At first I had a tendency to pull back on the controls while passing through the uncertainty of inversion, but the consequent sudden dive and increase in speed tended to discourage a second similar mistake.

The barrel roll is not quite as simple. Books by Kerschner and Cole disagree on the nature of this seemingly rudimentary maneuver. The problem is that the roll looks vastly different when viewed from the inside than from the outside. The ground observer sees the plane flying a horizontal spiral with the plane's wheels rolling along the inside of an invisible barrel, hence the name. The pilot sees the nose rotating widely about a point. Cole stresses nose position, but Kerschner deals with the maneuver from the external point of view. I found myself becoming confused.

I solicited the advice of local pilots, but found none with recent experience with barrel rolls. This in no way stemmed the flow of advice, however. I would take my plane up and try out each vagrant suggestion, but after many altitude-losing, speed-gaining abortive rolls the truth became evident: Nose position and true position didn't go hand in hand. Nose position led by 90 degrees. The craft was at its highest point when it was halfway through the roll in the inverted position, quite contrary to the majority opinion of those who frequently fly the local hangar. Once I perfected it, the barrel roll became one of my favorites. The g's remained positive throughout, ranging from plus 2 or 3 at start and end to a plus ¼ or so at the top. I could do barrel rolls endlessly with my eyes shut or glued to the altimeter to check the rise and fall in altitude. In reality the barrel roll is nothing but a loop stretched sideways. If you compare a loop to the coil of a spring, then the barrel roll is a coil on the same spring that has been over-stretched.

I have passed over the loop intentionally, because it has always been easy for me. It's simply a matter of diving to a speed 20 percent or so over cruise speed, then hauling back on the stick until the world turns upside down and then rightside up again.

The path is far from circular, but it's easy to correct that problem by slacking off on control pressure at the top of the loop and round it out.

Most pilots will tell you that altitude can be exchanged for speed, and speed exchanged for altitude. The statement is generally true. Those same pilots will tell you that a little extra speed brings added safety. But quite the opposite is true when it comes to entering a maneuver called the split S. A fellow pilot and friend was killed recovering from a split S. It is possible that he entered it with extra speed, assuming that the speed gave him a margin of safety.

The split S is a simple move. Just roll until you are inverted and pull back on the stick for half a loop until the plane is again upright and flying in the opposite direction. It was a favorite move of World War I pilots.

Entered at cruise speed, 120 mph, a split S in Second Sweetheart results in a loss of about 500 feet. But entered at 150, Duster Whiskey uses up 1,100 feet before straight and level can be achieved! It is much more enjoyable to begin by aiming the plane upwards on a 45-degree angle, then roll upside down and complete the loop with no loss of altitude. Repeat the maneuver and you have a Cuban 8, a favorite of airshow pilots. Once the basic moves are learned, it is a simple matter to put them together to form new, seemingly difficult maneuvers. Half a loop plus half a roll forms an Immelmann, and four loops with a quarter roll on the down sweep of each makes a cloverleaf.

The International Aerobatic Club, or IAC, is the official organ of the serious aerobatic pilot. The IAC sponsors a number of contests each year, separating pilots into four categories ranging from Sportsman to Unlimited.

For some time I had been toying with the idea of entering competition to see how my self-taught skills measured up to the tutored variety. To get an inside view of the competition, I drove the 300 miles to Boulder, Colorado, home of the nearest chapter of the organization. The fellows were helpful, drawing out the maneuvers required for Sportsman competition, explaining the "box" and the scoring system. They also invited me to enter the Rocky Mountain Aerobatics Championships to be held nearby on Memorial Day, just two months away.

Fired with new purpose, I hurried home, bought 200 pounds of lime and drove out to my favorite practice area in hopes of talking the local rancher into letting me lay out an aerobatic box in his pasture. He was a tall gangly sort, with a handshake like a steel vise. "So you're the fella that's been doing the fancy flying up there!"

It sounded as if I were in for something heavy.

"You know you cost me a whole afternoon's work—had half a dozen neighbors over to help me out and here you come a flyin' over—couldn't get a lick of work out of them—just sat there and watched."

His name was John Steinle, and he was tickled to have me lay out the corners of the box—even asked me to swing over the ranch each time to waggle hello. We discussed some of my practice maneuvers and I quickly learned that his slow drawling manner hid a quick eye and sharp judgment. He told me my loops wobbled on top, my "fast" rolls never came out straight and that he didn't like it when I flew straight down. I answered that those "fast" rolls were called snaps, but that he was right on every other count.

For the next few weeks, John made a practice of calling me an hour or so after a practice session and giving me the benefit of his advice. His comments were always helpful and welcome—as welcome as was his greeting each time I flew past the ranch at ground level. He always heard me coming and would be outside wildly waving his Stetson. Once I surprised him on the corral fence—he stood up on the rails and waved his hat anyway.

The aerobatic box was 3,300 by 2,600 feet. A small out-house stood at one corner, a gravel pit at another. I marked the two remaining corners with lime and traced a dashed white line down the middle. The bottom of the invisible box was 1,500 feet above the ground—the top was 3,500 feet. The actual elevation of the ground was about 5,400 feet, and in order to make net altitude calculations easier, I made it a practice to pass by at ground level and set the altimeter at an even 5,000 feet. The bottom and top limits would then be 6,500 and 8,500 feet on the altimeter.

Putting ten maneuvers together without pause was not easy, but I finally was able to struggle through the Sportsman sequence without a major goof. Eventually I could even do all ten and stay within the confines of the box. Full of confidence, I filled out my entry form for the Boulder contest—and stumbled across a few unexpected regulations in the process.

In order to perform at an aerobatic contest, it was necessary to have a paid-up $300,000 liability policy, membership in the IAC, and a current low-level waiver from the Federal Aviation Administration. I tackled the last item first.

The accommodating folk at the District Office of the FAA set the time and place for the waiver flight. I had only a week to practice before demonstrating my capabilities over the east-west runway of a little-used airport north of town. The maneuvers I chose and the altitude I wished to use were my options. The FAA representatives would judge my competence to repeat the same maneuvers in front of a crowd. I chose to do the Sportsman routine at 1,500 feet, breaking frequently to climb for altitude. I staggered out of the Immelmann, and overrotated on the spin. The final snap roll was crooked as hell, so I just held the wings crooked, swung about in a turn and bored in for a low-altitude knife-edge followed by a point roll, then a hammerhead to reverse direction, followed by a dive to ground level and a climbing aileron-roll finale.

I swung around, slipped into a landing on the dirt strip, taxied over to the FAA officials and inquired if there was anything else they wanted me to demonstrate. They were all smiles and compliments. Later, when the waiver was being filled out, I asked for some helpful criticisms. The observers had noted the flaw in the Immelmann but thought everything else was fine. It was their first experience, too, with a low-altitude waiver—we didn't learn much from each other, but we enjoyed the exercise.

Within a week I was invited to put on an air show. Having the only aerobatic biplane inside a 100-mile radius may have had something to do with it. Then again, it may have been because I worked so cheap. I still didn't feel that my talents warranted a fee.

This invitation, however, was ideal. The faculty members of the college where I teach were holding an afternoon picnic and wanted me to entertain the group. Of the hundred or so that were expected to attend, only three or four were pilots. Of those, only one had done any aerobatics, and he was an understanding friend. The picnic was to be held at the Casper Boat Club, on Alcova

Lake, a site not conducive to low-level aerobatics. The club was on the south side of a narrow bay banked on each side by 500-foot-high hills. I decided to play it cool and stay 1,500 feet above the water except for a low-level nonaerobatic pass or two.

At precisely 2:30, I swung down over the lake at high speed, flew the length of the narrow bay, a few feet off the water, set the altimeter at an even 5,000 feet, then zoomed up well clear of the hills. At 1,500 feet I flew through the Sportsman sequence. It was old stuff by now and slightly boring. I climbed a bit higher and tossed out two rolls of toilet paper which promptly unrolled to form long vertical ribbons. A split S put me through the bottom string, and a hammerhead reverse let me approach the top one on a climbing line. I rolled my way through the paper. I was tempted to dive straight down through the remainder, but feared that I might accidentally clog the air intake. Down below, the loud-speaker proclaimed that the toilet paper was not only biodegradable, but it was used, probably by the pilot. After one last pass at the toilet paper, pretty well bunched up by now, I swung down for a final flyby. I could see cars stopped on the road above. People were standing by their cars looking down at the plane several hundred feet below. The Sweetheart climbed nicely, speed dribbling off to a comfortable 100 as I leveled with the hill to my right. Suddenly I was smitten with a bright idea. I eased over the hill in a crippled altitude, then retarded the throttle as much as I dared, pulling the old disappearing act. I glided silently down the valley, out over the lake, and turned toward the Boat Club. Then, with throttle opened wide, I tore past the Boat Club again. I thought it was a great act—better than the one Bob Hoover does at Reno. Then I realized that my wife was in the crowd. The fun I had wasn't worth the scare she got or the hell I caught!

Requests for air shows poured in—both of them arrived the same day. The first offer was from students of the fourth-grade class in one of the Casper schools. The class had been studying a unit on aviation and wished to top it off with the real thing. With great regret I turned down the offer, since aerobatics over town were prohibited and an alternate site could not be found. The second offer was from a nearby small town that would pay gas money and a few extra bucks for a demonstration. I accepted immediately.

55

Looking back on it, I can see that my debut as a performer was something less than spectacular, but at least I knew that things could only get better. And I was now absolutely determined that some day I would fly for a crowd—a big crowd. The Starduster's potent magic had fired my imagination. Doubtless I was—and am—still the same rather humdrum fifty-year-old school teacher I had been when the Starduster entered my life. But I sure as hell didn't feel like it! I felt more like the Red Baron out on a foray.

5/Cutting the Umbilical

Of the many regulations laid down by the Federal Aeronautics Administration, relatively few apply to homebuilt aircraft. However, one of them caused me great frustration. The rule states that for the first fifty hours, a homebuilt craft may not fly more than fifty miles from home base.

I had already logged forty hours while testing the plane and learning basic aerobatics. Since those efforts were made close to home, the fifty-mile umbilical had never been a problem. But now with summer approaching, I had the urge to go places. Now, like a dog on a chain, I paced the perimeter, learning more than I really wanted to know about the terrain within the circle. Ten hours doesn't sound like much, but at 120 mph it meant 1,200 miles of wandering—always within the limits of my federally regulated playpen.

I looked at cows and sagebrush, creeks and lakes, and waved at countless fishermen. I flew up smooth slopes and down the precipitous canyons. Perforce, I investigated the haunts of eagles and the places where antelope play.

In fact, observing wildlife, especially from a height of a dozen feet or so, may have been the most fun I had. Their reactions to the passage of what must have seemed a big noisy bird were varied and fascinating. Dozing antelope reacted with total confusion. An entire herd would jump and run outward like a starburst. But wide-awake antelope were a different matter. Flying over undulating ground, the plane could be heard by antelope long before it could be seen. They are a most inquisitive animal, and the sound puzzled them. On several occasions I approached a rise to find an antelope standing on its hind legs, peeking over the rise to spot the source of the mysterious sound.

One early morning I happened upon two buck antelope fighting on the flat top of a broad mesa. Their heads seemed glued together as they took turns pushing each other about. They had been at it for a while, if the radiating scuff marks were any sign. I circled above and watched the proceedings. Finally, when the action slowed, I dropped quietly down to ground level, then opened the throttle wide as I passed overhead. Looking back, I could see two dust trails extending in precisely opposite directions. Each animal thought the other had won.

Bird watching is fascinating sport, and I admit to the hobby without shame. I prefer to do my watching from an aircraft, but it's tricky business. Buzzards are generally docile, and interpret the plane's presence as one more bird in competition for the food below. At times I have joined their spiral at high altitude, then left abruptly to circle about another spot, trying to lure them away. It seldom works, and then only briefly. The buzzard is a very smart bird.

Geese are spooky and quite intolerant. Flying in a slow aircraft, it is always sporting to attempt to join up at the tail end of the vee. The tail-end Charlie lets you approach just so close before squawking out a warning. Sometimes the lead goose fails to respond, the signals from the rear overwhelmed by the engine noise, but the message is relayed eventually and the vee breaks away, generally diving toward the ground and safety.

Eagles flap their wings with great majesty. Da Vinci would have delighted in a study of their movement. The main portion of the wing is always half a beat ahead of the tip, giving the wings a rubbery look, with elbows still rising as tips begin their descent.

But the eagle is not to be trusted. There are many eagles, both bald and golden, in Wyoming, and I've learned to leave every one of them alone. Where a hawk might veer away when approached, an eagle is more likely to close in belligerently. After all, he knows he's the biggest bird in this part of the world and therefore has no reason to fear. The first few times I pulled alongside an eagle, I thought his sudden approach was accidental. Then I began to keep track of their behavior carefully and found that while a few may fly away, most are inclined to close in, and some are instantly angry and aggressive.

But observing wildlife, fascinating as it was, eventually began to wear thin. The confinement caused by my 50-mile umbilical took the edge off even my more interesting local adventures. There came a time when radio conversations with traffic controllers in the local tower became the high point of most flights.

Each controller seemed to broadcast his own attitude by implication or inflection. It was like studying a new form of sedentary but vocal wildlife. One of the fellows could be called the drawler, or perhaps the gargler. He always spoke with the mike close to his lips. His voice could put you at ease in an emergency, or perhaps sound asleep on final approach. Occasionally he sounded as if he were running down and needed rewinding. I pegged him as a tall, friendly sort.

Some controllers are brusque and all business. One such broke in abruptly one day as I slowed after a landing. "One November Whiskey, go to ground." (rapid-fire)

It took a few moments to figure out that he meant I should switch to the ground-control frequency. "Casper ground, this is Starduster Whiskey." (slow, cool drawl)

"What did it cost to make that plane?" (staccato)

"Something over five thousand dollars," I answered, one syllable at a time.

"Probably worth it," he snapped, making it sound like all one word.

One communicator seemed to have a built-in bias against experimental aircraft. He always made me feel as if I were intruding upon his private air space. He was on duty one late afternoon as I approached for a landing. Traffic was light, but he was "busy." On the third call he acknowledged my existence, cleared me to land and went on to more serious matters.

"Western flight five cleared to take off. Traffic is a home-built [sneer] one mile south."

"Casper Tower, Western five. What make is the homebuilt [respect]?"

"Don't know. Just a homebuilt [sneer]."

"Would you ask the pilot?"

I broke in, volunteering, "Starduster."

There was a long pause before the controller replied. "Well, his call letters are Starduster One November Whiskey—guess it's a Starduster [smaller sneer]."

"Casper Tower, Western five. I have him in sight—it's a pretty bird."

On subsequent transmissions I made it a practice to refer to myself using such terms as CUSTOM-BUILT, SPORT PLANE, TWO-WINGER and finally, PRETTY BIRD. The controller finally got the message. After that it was a "biplane" or "experimental" (with only a trace of sneer).

One fun-loving operator gave the following instructions to a pilot, obviously a stranger, approaching for a landing: "Your clearance was for runway two-one—you are approaching runway three. Be advised that you will have a 40-knot tail wind; however, you may land on runway three if you wish." Nothing like creating a little excitement with a wild downwind landing on a dull day.

Low-level approaches to busy airports are generally discouraged. However, there are exceptions. When a new radar system was installed at the local airport, the newly trained operators frequently asked arriving pilots to take part in a mock radar approach. I always refused, explaining later that since the plane lacked any blind-flight instruments, I would never be able to penetrate an overcast anyway. However, since I could imagine that I just might someday have to come limping in under an overcast, glued to the ground, and unable to find the airport, I did ask if they could help me in such a case. John Chase, traffic controller, radar operator and transplanted Okee, figured he could find me on the scope and lead me in, no matter what my height. After all, he could spot passing trains on his radar scope, and he shrewdly suspected I couldn't fly much lower than that. I, on the other hand, doubted that he could find my blip among the ground reflections. We discussed the problem through half a dozen cups of coffee.

John happened to be on duty a few days later when I was making an approach to land under clear blue skies with 60 miles visibility.

"Say there, Duster Whiskey, when do you want to try that low-level radar approach?"

"How about right now?" I answered.

"But I can see where you are," came the drawling reply.

"Give me ten minutes," I countered, opening the throttle and heading for the hills southwest of town. Over the hills I dropped low, out of sight where the radar couldn't follow, then cut hard left for a few miles, caught the Platte River and headed downstream, back toward town, 20 feet over the water.

"Casper tower, Starduster One November Whiskey—I'm having trouble finding the airport. This imaginary ceiling has me pinned down low, and I can't see a thing. Can you help?"

"Duster Whiskey. We don't have you on the scope. Can you describe the terrain?"

"Well, there's some water now and then, some trees, and a house just went by." I stayed low, hidden behind the intervening hills, making John's work as difficult as I could. The hills flattened, and I could see the tower. That meant the radar could see me.

"Duster Whiskey, we have a blip. Give us a slow count to five and back."

John was sharp. He had Flight Service all set to put their direction finder on me. Seconds after I finished my count, John was back on the horn, very matter of fact.

"We have a positive identification. Make a left turn to three-five-zero."

I tried, but my compass swung all about. Besides I was busy dodging houses and a radio tower.

"Now take a right to three-zero degrees."

I made a sloppy stab at it, explaining my problem with the compass. John shifted gears, giving me instructions to bear right, then hold heading. His eyes were glued to the tube as he gave final directions.

"Bear right more. Hold your heading. Runway two-one is just ahead. Be ready to turn left and land."

At twenty feet above the ground, all I could see ahead was a grass-covered slope. "Nothing in sight yet, John. You sure there's a runway around here?"

"You'll see it just above the next rise," he answered, and I knew he had moved from the tube to visual, satisfied that he and the radar had performed their proper function.

And there it was, runway 21, right on the numbers. I passed over in a turn, swung back, straightened and landed. After parking, I climbed the long steps up to the tower and offered my congratulations. Then, on the way back, it suddenly dawned on me: I had logged my fiftieth hour! A little paperwork with the Feds, one more inspection and we would be FREE!

I stopped by the local GADO to ask John Montebello for an immediate inspection. (GADO—that's General Aviation Distric Office. Aviator types are heavily into abbreviations.) John's schedule would allow him to stop by the hangar the next day for final inspection, but in the meantime he suggested we get the paperwork out of the way. I could never quite keep up with all the forms required. John, being the cooperative sort, always kept me up to date and legal.

We finally worked our way down to the last paper, the Operations Limitations. That one surprised me. I had been flying as if there were no limitations, and now we were going to establish what the plane could or could not do. The matter was somewhat negotiable. John wanted to list all the separate maneuvers. I claimed the list would be too long. He wanted to try anyway, but on the twenty-second maneuver, he ran out of space, gave up and agreed to a simple statement to the effect that N1NW was allowed all maneuvers except vertical turns.

The inspection the next morning was routine—much simpler than the paperwork. John wanted to know all about the broken exhaust, and the dog hair in the carburetor. He checked vital items with great care, then signed the Airworthiness Certificate. (Now there's a term that should be abbreviated!)

The day was young, and it was time to taste my new freedom. I had been planning a particular trip for weeks. It wasn't a long jaunt, but it was beyond the old 50-mile limit by 30 miles—enough to stretch the umbilical and snap it properly.

The Schiffers and their two children live on a ranch tucked away at the mouth of a deep canyon. The hills rise hundreds of feet on either side of a small flat meadow that fronts the canyon like the flare of a trumpet. I had fished the area frequently over the past several years, and occasionally the Schiffers had driven into Casper for some of their fish (fried) and a check on the plane's progress. They had yet to see the plane fly.

From half a mile away I could see Tony walking across the yard. I bored in full throttle and roared overhead at 500 feet. On the turn around I could see Mary, the kids, the hired hand and his youngsters all tumble out to watch. I passed over on knife-edge at close to 1,500 feet, then hammerheaded a turn and came over again in a slow roll.

A few loops and snaps later, I sidled in at half-throttle and minimum altitude and threw out half a dozen candy bars, each with a 6-foot ribbon attached. On the return pass I could see the kids clustered about the point of confectionery impact. They were looking up, waving the ribbons. I waved back with the wings, waggled the rudder and pointed my Freedom Machine's nose for home, feeling very good inside.

My world was expanding. Thoughts of distant travel blossomed into lines drawn on excitingly unfamiliar maps. Having recently been intrigued with Steinbeck's *Travels with Charley,* I couldn't wait to lay out my own plan for travels with Second Sweetheart. Whereas Steinbeck had driven along the perimeter of the country, I would fly the heart of America, from coast to coast and border to border. I would fit in an aerobatic contest or two, a fishing trip to Northern Saskatchewan and maybe a week at the big airplane extravaganza at Oshkosh, Wisconsin. Perhaps I could touch the East Coast at Kitty Hawk, where the Wrights flew. Along the way I could trace the paths the old-time mail pilots flew, and maybe make a detour to Death Valley and roll my wheels along its dusty floor.

All those many dreams, long on the shelf, could now be

dusted off and polished. With Second Sweetheart I could fulfill them all. But first a shakedown cruise was in order.

South was the direction to travel. Since spring would already be greening the land, and since I had relatives and friends in Boulder and Colorado Springs, the route of the shakedown cruise was obvious. My chute was due for repack, so a brief stop along the way to Cheyenne was in order. Then I would go on to Boulder for an overnight with sister Jess and brother-in-law Ed; distance, 260 miles. The next day I could hop the short 80 miles on south to Colorado Springs for an overnight with Mike and Suzy Herbison, longtime backpacking friends. The trip back would require one fuel stop at Laramie, the midpoint on the route to Casper. Weather permitting, the trip would cover just over 600 miles in five hours' flying time spread over three days—a leisurely jaunt.

A westerly wind was blowing 40 knots, gusting to 50, the morning of my departure. Two line hands held down the wings as I taxied to runway 21 and faced into the wind. The wing-walkers trotted alongside briefly, then "hand launched" me and Second Sweetheart into the swirling air.

Seventeen minutes after takeoff, the Starduster and I sailed over Douglas, Wyoming, headed due east at 12,000 feet, traveling at a ground speed in excess of 180 mph. The air was cold at that altitude, but that was the altitude where Casper Flight Service claimed the strongest tail wind would be found.

The cockpit heater was full on. My feet were warm, but cold air washed over my left shoulder and curled behind my neck. After a lifetime of assuming that the old-time pilots wore scarves as an affectation, I abruptly realized that it was a perfectly practical idea. I stuffed my handkerchief under the helmet and hunkered my neck down.

Laramie Peak, more than 10,000 feet high, passed off the right wing as we slowly changed course to the south. Cheyenne was faintly visible 80 miles ahead, and Second Sweetheart was running smooth and free. The sky was cloudless and we were alone. I had forgotten how pleasant cross-country flying could be. No road to follow, no hassles, no press of traffic. The little plane provided the ultimate escape from an ever-compounding life on the surface.

Thirty miles out we began the long slope down to the runways of Cheyenne Municipal Airport, quartering a bit to cancel the effects of the west wind. Dwane Carey was waiting at the Air National Guard Hangar. We trundled the Sweetheart inside and tucked her under the wing of a gigantic airborne troop carrier. Uniformed personnel gathered around. She would be in good hands while we drove to Dwane's home for the chute repacking.

Stretched out, the chute was nearly 50 feet long. It had been satisfying to pull the ripcord and have the loaded spring fire the pilot chute out—proof that Dwane's earlier pack job was flawless. Within half an hour the chute was inspected, refolded, cocked like a set trap and carefully crammed back into its corset-like case.

Shortly, we were back at the hangar, and with the willing help of Wyoming's Air National Guard, the plane was rolled out and started up. Takeoff was spectacularly short against the brisk westerly. Climbing out steeply, I waggled a thank-you to the fellows now lined up across the cavernous mouth of the huge hangar. Along the row, uncountable hands waved back.

The wind died at the Colorado-Wyoming border. We stayed low, dodging the small towns that became more frequent as we sped south along the east shoulder of the Rocky Mountains. Visibility dropped to a few miles as we encountered the northern drift of Denver's smog. It surrounded us like a brown sickness, reducing the sun to dirty orange.

Ten miles from Boulder, I tuned the radio to 122.8, the frequency common to uncontrolled airports. The apparently empty sky became filled with pilots crowding the airwaves with intentions to land here, take off there and otherwise approach or overfly some particular point. There was no pause big enough for me to state my plans, so I drove in at ground level, spotted the planes in Boulder's traffic pattern, climbed quickly to fill an empty slot and followed the leader in to a landing.

While waiting for relatives to arrive, I was accosted by a chunky red-haired fellow, obviously a pilot type, who wanted to know if the plane ought not to be hangared rather than tied out. He had his own private hangar, he said, sort of a "foam dome" that just happened to have a space that needed filling. We traded names—his was Mike Ryer—then trundled the plane down the taxiway to the open door of the hangar and into some pretty fancy company. There was a Pitts single place on the right (Ryer's plane), and a scaled-down Bücker on the left (his wife's plane), along with two other single-place aircraft parked at each side of the door. Second Sweetheart was to visit that hangar frequently over the next few years.

It was bright and blue the next morning. The Denver smog had yet to spread. My sister and brother-in-law, Jess and Ed Kellenberger, helped ease the plane out of the closely packed hangar. Jess admired the plane and ran her hands over the smooth fabric, while Ed, with unlit cigar tucked at one side of his mouth, expressed doubts as to the plane's safety. Soon I was off, climbing steeply, waving back to Jess, who was no doubt telling Ed he should have more confidence in his in-laws.

Between Boulder and Colorado Springs lies a hazard called the Denver Terminal Control Area. Shaped like an inverted wedding cake smacked down on Stapleton International Airport, it offers a haven of control to airliners and other business types, but is pure hell for those flying sport aircraft with minimal radio facilities. It is legal, but a bit tricky, to fly the 700-foot-high gap between the ground and the middle layer of the cake. The ground rises frequently, threatening to block the path. Just west of Denver that possibility comes perilously close to fact. However, if one's mental attitude is proper, it can be fun snuggling up to the foothills of the Rockies, flying the valleys between ridges, detouring around small suburbs and carefully dodging all the towers with their invisible wires.

The cake layer ended just past Castle Rock, a dozen or so miles south of Denver. Here it was legal to rise to higher altitude, which was fortunate, since the ground ahead rose almost 2,000 feet. The high, tree-covered area was called the Black Forest, and was just north of my destination, Colorado Springs.

The lone runway of the Black Forest Glider Port seemed to be jammed up against the southern border of the forest. The runway sloped strongly downhill to the south. The slope was not detectable from the air, but luckily a friend had briefed me on the situation. It seems that everyone lands to the north, uphill, and takes off south, downhill. I circled the field several times, making

66

sure that I wasn't interfering with glider operations, then curved in and landed north, uphill, and of necessity, downwind.

I was given a warm welcome, for little bipes seldom dropped by. A small crowd gathered around the plane and one youngster asked to sit in the cockpit, then several more followed in turn, lifted in and out by grinning fathers. Each disappeared down in the depths of the seat, head below the level of the coaming, eyes on a level with the grip on the stick. By the time Mike and Suzy Herbison showed up, every youngster within two miles had "flown" Second Sweetheart.

Suzy raises Labs, and for years had tried to sell Jay and me one of her pups. Finally, in frustration, she gave us one of her prize pups—one of the smaller ones. That was two years ago, and Blue now weighed eighty pounds.

Mike's favorite Lab of the several around the house was a gentle giant named Bear. Mike had taken Bear along on a recent backpack and was strong on the advantages of four-legged companionship. However, there could be problems—like the one Bear created in the mountains just west of town.

It seems that old Bear had spotted a troop of Boy Scouts coming down the trail and took off to investigate. Mike tried to call him back, hollering "Bear, Bear!" The Scouts, hearing Mike yell and glimpsing the black form through the underbrush, quickly took to the trees, passing on the warning, "Bear, Bear!" Even the scoutmaster scrambled to safety. In seconds, "Bear," the friendly Lab, had treed the entire troop!

The sky was overcast the following morning. The sun squeezed a few rays through a crack in the eastern clouds and lit the face of the front range briefly. Sparse patches of blue appeared as I battled my way through the Denver TCA, then headed on for Laramie.

Laramie showed up on schedule, exactly an hour and a half out of Colorado Springs. After a brief contact over the radio, we curled in for a landing and a bit of fuel. She took 9.9 gallons, yielding an average of 19 miles to the gallon—cheaper than driving the car!

The usual small crowd had gathered about the plane as it was fueled. I stood at the fringe and listened to the comments, swelling immodestly with pride. It's a strange feeling. All the attention is directed to the plane, and none to its builder. But then the plane is beautiful, and I'm borderline ugly. Even when I shoulder my way to the cockpit with a polite "excuse me," I'm only tolerated. Reluctantly I'm permitted access, and begrudged a share of credit. Things change when I climb in and strap up. Now we are one. When I talk on the radio I'm "Starduster One November Whiskey." I have become an airplane! And at times like this I'd rather be an airplane—especially a little red and white biplane!

The same wind that helped me at the trip's onset now blew from the nose, reducing the ground speed to less than 100 mph. I lowered to a few feet off the ground to take advantage of the small reduction in head wind due to ground friction. Ground effect also offered an advantage. The air seems to compress between wing and ground, increasing lift and permitting some forward stick to be applied to offset the tendency to climb. The net result is extra speed. Theoretically, ground effect shows up only when the plane is within one wing span of the ground, but I would swear that it can be felt as high as 40 feet, more than two wingspans for the Starduster. Of course, there is a price for the added speed. One has to remain owl-eyed for hazards—particularly man-made hazards like power lines. Constant surveillance right and left is required to spot the poles supporting wires that may become visible too late.

Yet I confess I love that feel of speed that comes only when you fly a plane at low altitude. At 100 feet you begin to feel it; at 50 feet it becomes thrilling; and at 10 or 20 feet the madly unreeling ground produces—in me, anyhow—an exhilaration bordering on euphoria.

And it's not really as dangerous as it looks. A plane gives you three ways to escape a possible collision: right, left and up. In a car, if you can't turn, you can only try to stop in time. I am convinced that flying 10 feet above the ground at 130 mph in an aircraft is safer than driving 50 mph on the highway.

The Union Pacific tracks moved over to join our path. We flew by rail for a while, navigating by "iron compass." In bad weather, traveling by rail can become a necessity. Old-time mail pilots frequently flew the tracks, always keeping to the right to prevent a head-on collision with the fellow pilot flying the return route.

Stories about the early airmail service had been in the news for the past few months. It was the fiftieth anniversary of Western Air Express, a forerunner of Western Airlines. Airmail flying had actually begun seven years earlier along the Eastern routes. Of the forty pilots originally hired, only nine were alive six years later. They called it the "Suicide Club," and Lindbergh was one of its surviving members. The job paid $1,000 a month, a fantastic wage for the times.

In spite of the available space, company rules forbade passengers. Will Rogers promptly broke the rule and set a precedent by mailing himself—even licked the stamps and plastered them all over himself.

Shirley Mountain passed on the left, and the Laramie Range sidled in on the right. Flat ground was below, so we continued at low level, still fighting the wind. No power lines here— just fences and windmills, cattle and thousands of antelope.

Thirty miles out of Casper, we overtook an old beat-up Aeronca plowing along at 80 mph. The TE on the tail looked familiar. We moved in at reduced speed and waited to be noticed. Soon the pilot did the expected double take, then broke out in Stan Laurel-type surprise. It was an old rancher-pilot friend—a fellow named Bob Palmer, a questionable rancher, but an accomplished pilot. He signaled "2-2-9" with his fingers, and I turned to 122.9, the plane-to-plane frequency. His transmission arrived loud and clear.

"Hi-yah, Nit Wit." (He never dignified me or the plane with "November Whiskey.") The insult, however friendly, was meant to include his evaluation of my IQ, and, at the same time, exercise some of the words in his private phonetic alphabet. "F-L" was fruit loop, "C-C" was Canadian Club, "R-T" became Rat Trap and "R-S" was unprintable. The N1NW on Second Sweetheart's fuselage had always meant "Number One Nit Wit" to Palmer.

"Hello, Plumber. How's your conduct?" No true friend ever called Palmer by his right name—he would have been insulted.

"Impeccable," he replied. "I see that two-winged excuse for an airplane is still chewing up perfectly good air."

"Yeah, and chewing it about 50 miles faster than some slow-flying antique air knockers I've met." Before he could answer, I pushed in full throttle and moved ahead in a long slow aileron roll. As the wings leveled, I keyed in a parting shot. "Eat your heart out, Plumber."

Shortly, we began the descent into Casper. Muddy Mountain slid by a few hundred feet below as I made contact with the tower. The trip was nearly over. Everything about the shakedown cruise had been enjoyable—not a single problem had arisen. I longed to fuel up and head out on a longer journey, but there were plans to be made and duties to be performed.

The last weeks of the semester must be finished up, and I still had to grind through the chore of correcting final tests. I hoped the time would pass quickly, but I suspected it would not, for I was wild to get back into the air again. The freedom I had begun to experience in the Starduster was working on me like some narcotic drug. My little trip to Colorado Springs had been only a foretaste. Now I was ready for a more grandiose adventure.

6/Checking the Country for Leaks

The morning sun paled as lowering clouds enveloped Second Sweetheart in shadow. The cockpit became suddenly cold. A tug on the heat control brought the temperature back to reasonable comfort, but did little to improve the ominous view ahead. A solid layer of gray rode above me, reaching all the way to an indistinct horizon. Casper, now 50 miles behind, still enjoyed the sun on this uncertain day, the 22nd of May.

Small, ragged wisps of cloud began to appear underneath the leaden ceiling. Soon they multiplied to form a new stratum, forcing me to drop still lower toward ground level. The bottom of the cloud layer was now 6,500 feet above sea level, but the ground itself was 6,000 feet and rising, claiming more and more of my 500 feet of airspace.

The Buzzard Ranch materialized just over the Starduster's nose. A gentle bank, and the buildings passed to the left, only slightly below. A ranch hand on horseback leaned back, one hand on the horse's rump, his head swiveling as I passed. Ahead, the approach to the pass between the Ferris and Seminoe mountains was cut short where the ground rose to make contact with clouds. It was time for a discretionary 180. The lone rider waved, and I knew his thoughts—what's that damned fool up to, flying in this weather? I wiggled my wings: If I failed to show up at my destination, he might remember and contribute a clue to my whereabouts.

Rock Springs, Wyoming, was the first destination listed on my flight plan. The intended route had been by way of Ferris, an old town that I wanted to view from overhead, but with the pass blocked, the side trip to Ferris would have to be cancelled. Perhaps Rock Springs might also be unreachable. With thousands of miles ahead, I was in trouble in the first hundred. I wondered if my plans to fly from coast to coast and border to border were realistic.

Flying in the sharp wedge between cloud and rising ground would ordinarily be unsettling, but this was familiar territory. Soon the Sweetwater River appeared, and shortly the rounded top of the pioneer landmark Independence Rock passed below. A left turn, and I was above the highway heading south. The ceiling had risen to a luxurious 800 feet. The west edge of Ferris Mountain curved behind.

The clouds ahead were alive and changing, which signaled turbulent air hiding beneath. Brighter skies to the left invited a change in destination. On the third call, Rawlins Flight Service answered.

"Skymaster—ah, ah—one—ah—Whiskey, say your position again."

"Rawlins Radio, this is *Starduster* One November Whiskey, five south Lamont. What is your weather?"

"Ah, Skymaster One November Whiskey, we have one thousand feet and six miles, rain in western quadrant."

"Okay, I'll come on in. Looks bad over toward Rock Springs. Change my flight plan to your destination, please, and ah— that's *Starduster,* as in biplane."

Twenty minutes later, with a second radio contact, I received the altimeter setting, wind direction and a caution, "We have had antelope on the runway. Be advised of the hazard."

Twenty or so antelope stood beside the approach end of the runway, well-behaved and undisturbed by the intrusion. The left wheel touched gently, and immediately the right. Tail high, Second Sweetheart rolled straight and true down the blacktop runway. A left turn and the engine wound to a stop as the plane coasted to position beside the gas pump. There wasn't a soul on the ramp. There never is when you grease it in.

The flight had lasted exactly one hour and had consumed 6.4 gallons of gas. It figured out to be nearly 20 miles to the gallon. the tank held 22.5 gallons. At 6.4 gallons per hour, I could stay up for nearly 3½ hours. At 120 mph, the little biplane could go an impressive 400 miles, a range in excess of my kidney capacity.

The modified flight plan that had unexpectedly landed me in Rawlins was part of a much larger—if ill-defined—enterprise. In fact, a certain lack of definition was an essential part of the undertaking. I wanted to prove that the Starduster and I really had escaped the world of man-made rules, that we could go anywhere and do anything. And part of that proof would lie in our not being tied to exacting schedules and inflexibly plotted routes. I wanted to take the Starduster on a series of long cross-country hops. In general, I thought the shores of the Pacific Ocean might be a good first destination. But who could tell? Along the way we might have a change of heart and head for Mexico or Canada instead. The point was to improvise, to depend on nothing but our combined abilities—in a word, to be free.

The Rawlins Flight Service reported that the weather to the west was deteriorating. Rock Springs had rain in all quadrants. To the south, Grand Junction, Colorado, had unlimited ceilings with scattered clouds. South was the only choice.

The Sierra Madres of southern Wyoming occupied the left horizon. Scattered showers stretched out along the intended path, a minor irritation to be endured in pursuit of "sunny" Grand Junction—but there was more enduring than planned. The scattered showers merged to a general, inescapable light rain. Threads of water streamed across the fabric of Second Sweetheart's wings and trailed off in spray on each aileron. Rivulets formed on the windshield and crawled up to be blown away in the prop wash. A few drops curled inward to run down the inside surface of the windshield and drop on my hand holding the stick. About one drop every twenty seconds—not bad for an open cockpit, I figured.

Over Craig, Colorado, the rain ceased and the sun showed faintly through the thinning overcast. I passed over a station wagon going the same direction but at half the speed, gave a few quick wiggles of the rudder and zoomed to a dizzying 300 feet. Suddenly it was bright. Sunshine warmed my shoulder. The open cockpit let me feel its full effect. It was more than a fair trade: occasional raindrops for undiluted, heartwarming sunshine.

Hills rose on my right and left. They grew in size and our cruise altitude rose to match. Visibility in the rain-washed air was fantastic. Mountain crests 70 miles away were sharply defined. A deep canyon joined our path, opened up and offered a gentle, ever-widening approach to the single runway just east of Meeker, Colorado.

While I was refueling at Meeker, a pilot who had just arrived from Grand Junction offered a disappointing description of the weather. He had come up the Colorado River Canyon V.F.R. (visual flight rules) and had nearly given up and refiled I.F.R. (instrument flight rules) several times. He had squeaked under several thunderstorms that had since matured behind him, closing the canyon.

I waited an hour for the storms to clear, then headed toward the canyon, full of determination. But five miles south of town, the mouth of the canyon was obscured by a white curtain of rain. The route southwest, over high lands cut by deep canyons, seemed to be the safer path. The straight line distance was less than 40 miles. I headed across the rough country counting on 20 minutes of worry before the ground would lower and flatten.

The sky was a cold electric blue, shot with thousands of small, puffy clouds. To my right, the clouds diminished and became widely scattered, offering a possible escape route, but dead ahead, clouds threatened the heights I had to clear. Dodging right and left, pursuing the open path, I was just able to squeeze over the highest ridges.

The immediate danger was past, but my passage from ridge to valley was now bringing sudden changes in altitude. Even though I was flying level, my height above the ground was changing rapidly from 50 feet to 1,500 feet. Faint stirrings of the gut marked the return of my insipient fear of heights—a fear so strong that the thought of mountain climbing is a subject of my nightmares. Oddly, flying over reasonably level ground causes me no trouble. But over rough country my only defense is greater altitude, and the implied safety of an increased glide distance in case of engine failure. But here that comforting option was denied. The clouds hung tenaciously a few hundred feet over the canyon rims.

Twenty minutes later, when the hoped-for flat country had still failed to appear, it occurred to me that I must be off course, having unconsciously held to the right, toward the lesser cloud cover. A glance at the compass confirmed the suspicion. With a kick of the rudder, I swung the nose to a new, more southerly heading, and ten minutes later the flats of what had to be the Grand River Valley appeared below. I saw a four-lane highway reaching in from the left and near it a railroad and river winding their way southwest in nearly perfect synchrony. My detour had put me well north of Grand Junction. According to the air map, the highway below would turn west and lead me directly to the small airport of Green River, Utah.

The decision made concerning the next stop, it was time for a little relaxation. A slight side pressure on the stick and we were standing on a wing tip, then rolling and slicing down inverted. The plane stood momentarily on the opposite wing, then continued and rolled level in a mild dive. Slight back pressure had kept the g's positive, and the luggage had remained on the floorboards. The speed reached 160 mph and the wires began to sing. The sound and feel were intoxicating. Up we went, climbing sharply, then rolling slowly, the nose dropping, level again at normal cruise, then up and around again. I can't recall instigating the second roll, or the third. Like a bird given freedom, Second Sweetheart cut new, unexpected lines through the sky. I felt like a passenger—a delightedly surprised passenger privileged to be in company with such a rare spirit. She cared little about g's, negative or positive. The luggage rose off the floor and lodged under the crook of my knee. I held it in place with my left hand. My right was still on the stick, but only passively. I felt out her moves as Second Sweetheart curved through one more wide, weightless, falling roll.

The altitude was gone. We returned to normal flight and normal relationship. I was still the pilot, right? Now let's settle down before I get into trouble with the FAA.

Ahead, a double line of trees drew a green curve. The trees lined both banks of the river called Green. The small towns of Green River and Elgin occupied opposite banks. Green River, the larger of the two, was much like a miniature railroad layout. Main Street, the airport, the highway and the railroad were crowded into unnecessarily close quarters. Main Street seemed to meld, lose its buildings and become the east-west runway. The tracks of the railroad moved over and closely paralleled the air strip. As if on order, a train approached as I patterned for a landing. The engineer waved from the cab as I taxied back. I raised an arm and returned the salute. Ah, the joys of an open cockpit.

The east end of the strip was connected to the hangar area by a curving, down-sloping ramp. I cut the engine and coasted quietly down the hundred yards or so to the gas pump. The usual small crowd gathered as I unbuckled. I could see lips moving but could not catch the words. It's awkward being half deaf from the noise of the engine while confronted with a series of rapid-fire questions. I faked it a little, since the questions always seemed to follow the same pattern.

"It's a Starduster. Nope, it's not a Pitts. About a hundred and twenty." My hearing began its return as I dismounted and attached the Pitot tube cover. A man confronted me with an astonished look.

"You serious? It lands at a hundred and twenty?"

"Sorry, I'm a little deaf right now. It cruises at one-twenty and stalls about sixty."

He looked relieved.

Two youngsters, on tiptoe, leaned into the cockpit from opposite sides. One was explaining features to the other. Their heads bobbed in and out. A small controversy developed. One of them looked in my direction. "That is too a parachute ain't it? He says it's just seat cushions." The last comment was directed face to face across the cockpit.

My explanation that it served both purposes made them feel like experts. They continued their inspection, the conversation less one-sided now.

A car skidded to a stop. Half a dozen teenagers piled out and trotted over to the plane. "Boy, sure is purdy—what is it, a Pitts?"

"Nope," and I point my eyes toward the cowl, where it says STARDUSTER in large white letters. "It's a Starduster."

"Boy, single place, huh?"

"Yup."

"Well, one thing sure. You ain't never gonna get hijacked."

The oil was checked and the tanks filled. I decided to forgo lunch and continue on my way. It was only 12:30 and Las Vegas was just two gas stops away.

Ten minutes later I was not so positive about the destination. The horizon had again filled with thunderstorms. Virga hung from their flat undersides. It appeared that a route could be found between the hairy extensions of rain. I aimed the nose toward the area of least rain, but lightning immediately flashed from cloud to ground dead ahead. A new heading straight west put me on a course for Richfield, but more storm cells blocked the path. The lightning found new intensity as the sky darkened. To the north, storms formed a solid black ominous wall. I made the third 180 of the day and headed back for Green River. That line of thunderstorms could wreak its havoc without me.

Every experienced pilot has found his own severe storm. For most, it is the last, for to survive is to learn never to re-enter such an arena. My violent lesson was dealt me one summer day back in the late forties.

I was flying charter out of Park Rapids, Minnesota, headed for Minneapolis. The local beauty queen and a businessman were in the rear seat of the three-place Super Cruiser. The takeoff was a precursor of events to come. A suitcase placed in front of the stick had jiggled back on takeoff and caught against a metal floorboard plate. The suitcase, locked firmly in place, had in turn jammed the stick in its rearward, ground breaking position. I could not free the suitcase and we were climbing steeply. Forward speed deteriorated and a stall was imminent. I cranked in all the nose down trim available, and the speed held at a shaky 55. It held long enough for me to jam the suitcase forward with both feet. If the passengers noticed, they said nothing. The businessman was enjoying his seat beside the queen, and she was busy being thrilled by her first flight.

Midway in the flight I was forced down to 500 feet in order to pass under a ragged line of clouds, the sort of line often seen under maturing thunderstorms. But here there was no apparent storm, nothing to spawn such a line. We passed beneath the clouds and experienced only mild turbulence.

With passengers delivered and the plane refueled, I headed back along the same route. Minneapolis radio claimed that the weather was fair, and furthermore, that there should be a tail wind at 6,000 feet. The tail wind wasn't there, so I sat back and resigned myself to a slow return flight, wondering if that weird line of clouds would still be hanging over the lakes near Brainerd.

The line had moved and grown darker, but it still looked innocent. It had been safe an hour and a half before, and would surely still be passable, even though it was lower to the ground now, and there appeared to be some vertical motion. I proceeded beneath with a confidence born of ignorance.

All hell broke loose as severe turbulence suddenly hurled me about the sky. I took a quick yank on the seat belt and reduced throttle to ease the strain on the aircraft. At an indicated 70 mph, the bumps were still severe and seemed to be worsening. The seat belt bit into my hips on each rapid drop, and my chin sagged to my chest on the returns. At times the plane was rolled on its side. Full opposite control seemed to have no effect. The Cruiser would recover eventually from each half roll only to whip violently in the opposite direction. The trees below were waving like grain, and the wings of the poor old Cruiser were flexing up and down, pivoting on the strut attach points, moving nearly a foot at the tips. I knew the plane was lost and felt strong regret. For reasons I cannot now explain, the fact that I was lost with it seemed quite secondary. I continued to fight the controls. Heavy rain came with a rush. The windshield became a blur, and water flowed through the cockpit in small rivers. Visual contact with the ground had almost ceased, and I dropped lower, fighting to maintain control. Suddenly the air smoothed, and I realized I might still have a chance if I could find a place to land. But the trees formed a solid, frustrating barrier. I was now flying in a 45-degree crab. My air

78

speed was 90 mph and the wind must have been roughly the same velocity.

Below me a break in the trees flashed past, then a plowed field, and another. The second field was in line with the wind, and long enough for a landing. I headed for it. There was no mistaking the wind direction, for it was kiting the plane sideways. All I needed was to turn into it and set down on that inviting smooth brown surface. I touched and rolled, but I was much too fast. A fence loomed ahead. I jammed the throttle forward, soared upwards and went around for another try, slower this time. The plane touched, slowed and came to a stop. The ground was soft and had a slippery liquid feel. The wind was still blowing dangerously, well over the minimum flying speed of the Cruiser. I held half throttle, and with brakes hard on, flew it through each gust, tail high and stationary, locked in contact with the ground. Occasionally a wing would lift and a wheel threaten to leave the ground, requiring quick stick movements to hold position. Finally, after about ten minutes the wind slackened. I thought to look at the air speed indicator. It would now be acting as an anemometer: It was swinging between 40 and 50.

Slowly the rain eased, the wind diminished and the tail lowered to the ground. Now I could look around. I had landed in a freshly cultivated field. Small green shoots of wheat lay flat, battered to the ground by wind and rain. It was going to be difficult to take off from this sea of mud. I was too close to the fence to risk a straightaway departure, and the wind was still too strong to taxi. If I timed it right, I might be able to taxi to the down wind end of the field as the wind let up, then get off quickly before it died out altogether.

I gambled on a turn to a downwind heading, praying that careful manipulation of the aileron would hold the windward wing from rising. The wing lifted alarmingly, but finally we were around, facing downwind, stick hard forward. It took half throttle to move in the mud in spite of the following wind.

At the far end of the field I turned for takeoff, taking the same precautions with the ailerons. The tail rose as the plane faced into the wind. Wide open, we slowly gained speed. Mud flew from the wheels and clattered on the wing undersurfaces. I eased back on the stick. She lifted slightly, then sagged and slowed. A bump, and some mud dropped from the wheels. The plane lifted, then touched again. I jammed the stick forward, bouncing hard. Mud flew off the wheels and we bounced clear of the ground. She was flying, staggering with stick full back, but slowly gaining speed. A fence, a gravel road and a second fence were immediately ahead. We cleared the first fence, bounced hard on the road and were finally airborne. There was a farmhouse to the left. A man stood in the open door. I slanted my wing toward him, hoping he could not read the large numbers printed there.

The wind lessened, then died completely as I flew the remaining miles to Park Rapids. Tall clouds formed a half circle behind. The trees below were unmoving in the newly calmed air. It was as if nothing had happened. I was an hour late and the boss had been worried. I explained the delay, playing it down as much as possible, not ready to admit to the full fright I had experienced.

"Sure glad you weren't on the ground at Minneapolis. Just heard over the radio that a cyclone hit."

My God. I had flown through a *cyclone!* A dry land *hurricane!* It has grown to size and died, with Park Rapids all the while within its calm eye.

"Wiped out more than a hundred aircraft—Sure glad to see you." ⸱

Thirty years had not erased the memory nor dimmed the lesson of that storm. The prospect of a similar encounter hastened my retreat from the wall of thunderstorms in central Utah.

At midmorning the next day the skies were clear, the wind was calm and I was lost. Escalante should be right beneath me. The map on my knee showed the location clearly, and my watch said I had traveled long enough to have covered the distance. But there was nothing below except dry washes and eroded hills. Not even a road to follow or use as an emergency landing strip!

The map had not agreed with the land since Hanksville. The Boulder Mountains were still on the right, and Lake Powell somewhere on the left. I couldn't possibly be lost. Escalante was simply misplaced. There had been a reflection off to the right a few miles back, tucked away in a notch at the foot of the mountains, but that had to be the small town of Boulder. Escalante, on the map at least, was on a flat in front of the slopes, with a river

80

running through it heading east, cutting across my course. There had been no sign of a river, so I continued, confident even though the gas gauge was bouncing on the short side of the halfway mark. Twenty minutes later there was still no river. Nothing recognizable had appeared below. The gas level had dropped to the quarter mark and the engine was sounding rough. The little Lycoming didn't take kindly to the economy measures of lean mixture and low rpm's. I bent Starduster Whiskey around and took a course back to that small reflection noticed earlier. It was the only straw available, and it was time to start grabbing.

Starduster Whiskey's gas gauge is like the small tube that stands alongside most large coffee urns. Such gauges are very accurate and quite foolproof as long as no one shakes the urn. Bumpy air was sending the gas level up and down from one quarter to less than empty. Whatever happened to that three-hour range I had relied on? I had been airborne just two hours and the tank was nearly dry! I must have failed to fill the tank at Green River. Perhaps the gas spit back prematurely and the tank was assumed full. The gas in the tube leveled momentarily at the top of the letter "E" as I turned toward the mountain at whose base I had noticed a faint reflection. The reflection grew to a building. The buildings multiplied and resolved into a town, complete with an airport that had "ESCALANTE" painted on its runway in large orange letters! I approached high and straight in. The 22½ gallon tank took 21 gallons to fill.

It is 120 miles from Escalante to St. George, measured along a straight line. A short leg with plenty of gas reserve was welcome. The air was warm, and I climbed to a comfortable 10,000 feet, then to 12,000. The mountains on the right lost their sharpness and sank into the flattening earth. Small streams occupied seemingly flat valleys. The east fork of the Virgin River was the exception. It flowed nearly straight west at this point to pass eventually through the southern portion of Zion National Park. I followed the river to the park border, then swung north over the mountains to intercept the north fork of the Virgin River as it began its spectacular descent through the park's most impressive canyon.

From 12,000 feet, Zion was simply a bad case of erosion. From 10,000 it was a canyon, and at 8,000 it was a CANYON! We lowered, and the canyon walls rose and enclosed us. Water flowed straight toward the plane from breaks in the wall, then dropped in lacy fronds to the canyon floor. I circled, then regretted the move. People below were viewing the same beauty and would not appreciate our presence. I headed down the canyon, camera in hand.

Biplanes are not built for aerial photography. There is always a wing in the way. No clear view to the ground is available. I spent a lot of time on wing tip, holding course with rudder in wild knife-edged slips. Air poured through the cockpit from the wrong direction, and the altitude slipped away. I tried shooting through the windshield, over the windshield, and even clicked off a few exposures with the camera over my head aiming backward. Perhaps inverted, shooting down, which would be up, would be the best. In a biplane, the ways to waste film are limitless.

St. George unicom answered on the first call. There was no traffic, and the wind was calm. The strip occupied the flat top of a mesa at the edge of town. I entered high on the downwind leg, passed over the business district and curved sharply down in a slipping turn, straightened and flared over the numbers. Eight gallons of gas, a quart of oil, two cups of coffee and we were in the air again.

Soon the rough country southwest of St. George gave way to the broad valleys of the Virgin River, only to change again as desert took over the land.

A dozen or so miles out of Las Vegas, the highway curved past a small, dry lake. A small group of partially collapsed buildings huddled at the lake's perimeter. I swung down to investigate, and at an altitude of 300 feet the United States Air Force caught up with me.

Two delta-shaped shadows, sharply defined, raced over the ground directly below. I swiveled my head to locate the two aircraft responsible. From their shape and speed, they had to be jets. I resented the unfairness of the match: their 600 mph against my 120; their radar against my bifocaled eyesight. I checked my own shadow and found it to be less distinct than that of the jets. Those rascals had passed between me and the ground! I had been skylighted all the while. Well! Two could play that game. I promptly lowered to six feet off the dry lake. "Get under that!" I yelled. I scanned the skies waiting for their return pass, figuring to let them close in, then make a tight 6 g avoiding turn. They wouldn't have a chance of following. They would be out there five miles, skidding, trying to warp their big machines around for another pass. They didn't know it yet, but the little biplane and I could carry out formidable evasive action. We had the moves, and no modern-day Red Baron was going to get *us* in his sights.

I rose to twenty feet and took a quick look at my map. I had trespassed five miles inside the Nellis Air Force Base Alert Area; in fact, those long blacktop strips three miles off had to be the runways of Nellis. Good grief! Two more jets were rolling down the runway headed in my direction. Were these guys serious? Four against one! Well, it would take more than four. An entire squadron couldn't catch us where we were going.

I banked the Sweetheart hard to the left and ducked behind a low knob. A moment later, clear of the knob, I stole a quick look toward Nellis. The two jets were closing, their knife-edged wings parallel and low to the ground. I headed down the nearest dry wash full-bore, banking at each bend, wing tips within feet of the sides, the entire aircraft frequently below ground level. I scooted for the boundary and the shores of Lake Mead, telling myself it was all in fun, yet feeling melon-patch fear chase up my spine.

I climbed to 1,000 feet over Lake Mead, well out of the alert area, and reconsidered the encounter. The first pass was obviously intentional, but probably unplanned—just two bored jet jockeys out to scare the guy in the little red biplane. But the scramble of a second pair could hardly have been coincidental. I had probably been the practice intercept target for the day. In any case, both sides of the dry lake air battle learned a lesson. They learned that a jet can't catch a little biplane at the bottom of a crooked dry wash, and I learned to stay the hell out of their area.

It was cool and calm at the Boulder City Airport when I arose the next morning. I rolled up my sleeping bag, stuffed it in the baggage compartment behind the headrest, untied the wings and checked the tail rope to see that it was still tied securely. Two shots of prime, a dozen dry pulls on the prop and she was ready. With magnetos on "both," I stood between wing and prop. In one downward stroke the engine fired and settled into a confident chuckle. If there had been a crowd around, I'd probably have climbed in the cockpit, run the stick up my pant leg, strapped in and attempted to taxi away with the tail still securely tied down. But since there was no one about, I merely untied the tail, climbed in and ran the stick up my pant leg.

It was surprisingly hilly west of Las Vegas. The ground climbed rapidly, but in the cool air Second Sweetheart's rate of climb, nearly 2,000 feet per minute, let us top the Spring Mountains effortlessly. I continued west, threading the gap in the Nopahs, cutting across desolate country to a patch of green that had to be the town of Shoshone. There was an airport at this town, but reportedly no gasoline. I pointed the nose straight down the runway regardless. I was filing what is known as a poor man's flight plan. I passed down the strip at ground level, then rose normally at the north end, passed over Shoshone's small business district, made a turn in the intended direction, then flew a straight course out.

As a matter of fact, I had not filed an official flight plan since leaving Rawlins, and had no intention of doing so. To file a flight plan would have denied me too many of the pleasures of discovery. I could not tolerate the loss of freedom. But that doesn't mean that Second Sweetheart and I were unprepared.

In the otherwise empty wing-tank compartments were three gallons of water, two days' worth of dry food, a floppy hat, pack sack, compass, matches and a couple of paperback books. Beside me, in small compartments on either side of the seat, were the miniature smoke bombs, flares and an unbreakable signaling mirror. The last was most important, and I was well checked out on its use. Many pilots, I suspected, carried such an item with little idea of its use or effectiveness. It was a simple matter of looking through the hole in the middle and turning the mirror until the sun's reflection struck your outstretched finger while that finger was held in line with a would-be rescuer.

Five minutes west of Shoshone, I intercepted a blacktop road as it topped a low pass overlooking the south end of Death Valley. It meandered down and I followed, imitating each turn in an exercise of coordination. The hills fell away, and I broke abruptly into the open. Death Valley! The locals call it "The Monument." Flat, hot, lonesome and seemingly endless, it stretched north, disappearing in waves of heat. I wanted to travel its full 80-mile length and return by way of the paralleling Panamint Valley, but the added distance would press on my fuel reserve.

I headed north up the center of the Valley, searching for its lowest point, cruising at an altitude of ten feet. More altitude was unnecessary, for I could land anywhere. The gravel road beneath me offered a temptation. Carrying 1800 rpm, I eased down, the wheels touched briefly and a cloud of dust boiled behind. Again, and I turned to admire the rooster tail. A pickup was parked alongside the road ahead. I continued with little deviation, "filing another flight plan," and bending the FAA regulations in the process. I rolled the wheels again and slowed a bit, considering a full stop landing, then decided to settle for a touch and go.

Just ahead the road divided. A sign on the left fork read "Ballarat." Only short messages on such small signs could be assimilated at this speed. The map had this spot marked at −225, or 225 feet below sea level. Fifteen miles ahead was the lowest point in the continent, 282 feet below the sea. I looked carefully for wet spots. If the country were to spring a leak, it would show up somewhere nearby. At the low point, I found no water—just more barren sedimentary slopes. I concluded that the country was sound and in no danger of sinking.

The fuel gauge bounced a warning. I climbed over the rim and headed southwest. Inyokern was 30 miles west, but the China Lake Air Base and its surrounding restricted area lay across the route. To miss it would take 55 miles or 35 minutes' worth of gas—more if a head wind developed. I had started with full tanks and had been airborne for 2.3 hours. I should have .7 or .8 hours left—about 45 minutes.

I climbed out at 2,150 rpm, fuel mixture leaned to the maximum. Ten miles out, the fuel level still rode above the "E." I had been this route before. "Inyokern Unicom, Starduster One November Whiskey, ten southeast. May I have an advisory?" No answer. I gave the transmitter a few taps. "Inyokern Unicom, Starduster Whiskey, do you read?"

"Starduster Whiskey, this is Oh Five One. Can I help?"

"Oh Five One, Duster Whiskey here. I'm just looking for an airport directive and a little fuel."

"Starduster Whiskey, Oh Five One. I refueled there earlier. They didn't answer then either."

"Thanks. Where are you talking from?"

"I'm over the Monument, about eighty northeast of you. Your transmission is good. Just wanted you to know your problem is not in your equipment."

Nice guy. I wondered what Oh Five One looked like. I would like to meet him.

The fuel level rode just at "E" as the wheels contacted the runway at Inyokern.

Shortly, we were fat with gas and coffee and in the air again. The peak north of Garlock was listed on the map as 5,244 feet. Since I had failed to set my altimeter at the last stop, I pulled alongside, leveled the peak with the horizon and adjusted the altimeter to 5,244.

A quick stop at Mojave, and I was off again. Dodging restricted area No. R-2515 surrounding Edwards Air Force Base, I skirted the inland shoulder of the San Gabriel Mountains, then headed straight for Redlands, California. The sky over the San Bernardino Valley was a sea of white; solid, fluffy, beautiful, impenetrable white. Somewhere beneath was Redlands Airport and Lou Stolp, the designer of the Starduster aircraft. I circled over Arrowhead Lake in flawless sunshine, frustrated at my inability to drop through the overcast. I very much wanted to meet Lou Stolp and ask a few questions about the Starduster named Second Sweetheart, our mutual creation.

The man at Hisperia Air Park served a good sandwich, and was full of confidence. "You just fly down the highway. We all do it. Look out for those wires, though. Two or three sets of 'em. Never see the wires. Look for the towers."

I called the area Flight Service on the telephone. They were helpful, but annoyed with questions about a phenomenon that was for them a daily, monotonous occurrence. "Just drop through on the gauges. We have one thousand feet and several miles underneath."

I disclaimed ownership of any such gauges.

"What aircraft are you flying?"

At the mention of the name Starduster, the agent suddenly became friendly. "Tell you what you do. Wait until one-thirty; then head down the highway. Smog ought to be lifting by then. Look out for the transmission lines though."

At one-thirty I was off to do battle with the smog and the local utility company. The highway ahead dove into the mess and disappeared. With the map on my knee and my finger inching along, tracking my progress, I penetrated the smog. The world shrank to a hemisphere two miles in diameter that moved with me, revealing its secrets grudgingly. Faint images became towers and I climbed until the view below lost clarity in the haze. The world became smaller, a minuscule circle of dim visibility, moving at equal speed, remaining precisely below. The road descended. I followed, and the visibility improved. The world grew to a huge six-mile diameter. At 1,200 feet over the surface I followed a railroad south, took a left at the first airport and paralleled a four-lane highway east. Finally, Redlands east-west runway emerged on schedule, and after a brief radio conversation with the controller, I curved in on close pattern and landed.

From the grin on his face, as broad as the biplane grin that afflicts me when I strap up, I knew the man approaching was Lou Stolp.

"Nice landing."

"Thanks. It's a nice airplane."

He inspected the plane as it was fueled. A bolt was missing from the right wheel pant. "Push her over to the shop and we'll fix her up." His grin was still there. It was understandable. He had designed the aircraft some twenty years ago, built several, and later sold them. It pleased him to look at Second Sweetheart, and his pleasure was my compliment.

"Nice paint job. Enamel?"

"Yup. Dulux and TLC."

He was still grinning. Later we sat in his office at the airport and I asked him about cruise speeds, stall speeds and spin characteristics. Second Sweetheart was normal, but perhaps a bit slow. He suggested a little work on the propeller pitch, or perhaps a double check on the tachometer. It might be fooling me into cruising at low rpm. I decided to try a raise of 100 rpm.

Lou didn't like the idea of aerobatics and gently tried to discourage me. My explanation of the strengthening put into the plane brought no endorsement.

"You know, every friend I've ever had that went into aerobatics is now dead."

His feelings on the subject were personal. The aircraft was airworthy enough, Lou explained; it was the pilotage that was dangerous. We talked of many things. I listened and I learned. I complained about the smog, and extolled the virtues of Wyoming with its 60-mile visibility. Lou explained that the smog lifted a bit each afternoon, then socked in each morning. If I wanted to head east to the desert, I would have to leave soon or wait until noon the following day. So I said a premature, reluctant good-bye and headed out.

The higher cruise was a grand improvement. The engine was smoother and its pitch more intent. I couldn't tell if the tachometer was off or the engine simply smoother at the new setting. Either way, I liked the result. The needle of the air-speed indicator had found a new home 7 mph to the right of the old one, an improvement that might raise hob with my quick time and distance calculations. Figured by the old method, using a speed of 120 mph, I might constantly find myself arriving ahead of time— not a disappointing prospect.

Thermal, California, showed up ahead of schedule. We landed at 4:04, just twenty-nine minutes after leaving Redlands, 68 miles behind. That was more than 132 mph! Tie-downs secure, I patted Second Sweetheart with new affection and headed for the Flight Service Station.

None of us could figure out the map. The multitude of restricted, warning and alert areas on the map overlapped and compounded themselves into a mess we could not resolve. Reading the fine print pertaining to each area merely tangled the matter further.

It appeared that there was no easy, legal way to get from Thermal to Imperial. Other pilots gathered about, and one tall fellow volunteered that he always took the slot between the two restricted areas, through the MOA (Military Operations Area) straight to Imperial. I figured I would do the same and squared the details with FSS. The tall gent and I walked out the door together, diverging somewhat as we headed for our respective aircraft.

"That a Pitts?"

"Nope—Starduster."

"You're Starduster Whiskey!" He was looking at the plane, not me. "I talked to you up near Inyokern."

I glanced at the numbers on his plane and succumbed to like protocol. "You're Oh Five One. Glad to meet you. Appreciated your help." I've forgotten his face, but I can describe Oh Five One in detail.

Visibility over the Salton Sea was unlimited in all directions but one, straight ahead. It looked like smog, but billowed like blowing dust. At 5,000 feet over the ground I could taste its grit between my teeth. I rose to 6,500 to clear what I now recognized as a sandstorm. The extremely fine sand on low flats southwest of the Salton Sea must make such storms a common occurrence.

From my vantage point above the disturbance, I could make out the runway at Imperial, 35 miles ahead. The tower reported winds of 30 knots. Now 30 knots is nearly 40 miles an hour, and the wind direction and the runway heading were 90 degrees apart. I could imagine the guys in the tower elbowing each other with a "Watch this; thirty knots plumb crosswind, and that idiot's gonna try to land!"

Their communication with me showed no anticipation, however, only cooperation as they made sure I understood the perpendicularity of the wind by giving me permission to land in either direction on the lone runway. I lined Starduster Whiskey up on final approach, holding 30 degrees left heading to keep from being blown away. Over the threshold I dropped a wing and swung the nose in line with the strip. We drifted. More aileron, more rudder, and we still drifted. The wing was at such an angle now that it would be two feet underground by the time the upwind wheel touched.

"Thank you, Imperial. I guess we'll go on to Calexico."

Customs officials at Calexico did not recommend that I continue flight into Mexico. They mentioned certain special forms for experimental aircraft but had none available. Of course, they carefully stated, I could fly on if I wanted to discuss the matter with Mexican officials in Mexicali. But a dozen pilots had warned me about flying a homebuilt into Mexico. At Redlands, for example, I heard that a local pilot had flown his homebuilt into Mexico, filled out the required forms and, with their well wishes, flown south for a little fishing. He landed at the same airport on his return, as had been requested, to find that a slight problem had developed. The local authorities had found that aircraft licensed in the Experimental category could not legally be flown in Mexican airspace. His plane was confiscated. That was five years ago, and the Mexican authorities still have the plane.

Rather than snarl Second Sweetheart in red tape, I decided to skirt the border and head for Arizona. At least that was my intention. Five miles away and well into Mexican airspace, the runways at General Toboada International Airport offered a blatant, seductive welcome. I headed toward the airport, violating the border, wondering how close I dared approach. Discretion overcame desire, and I settled for a mild demonstration of disappointment. Firewalled, I nosed down until the speed reached 150 mph, then lifted in a high, wide barrel roll. At the top, completely inverted, I looked down on Mexico and offered a snappy middle-fingered salute, the international sign of recognition.

A brisk tail wind hustled us on our way. Yuma radio reported a strong tail wind two thousand feet higher. We climbed and sailed even faster, racing the sun to Gila Bend.

The sun was touching the horizon as we passed over Gila Bend. Time and our lowering altitude cooperated to sink the sun completely. We approached the runway flying into a rising sky of red and orange and yellow. On rollout, a tall Sugauro Cactus moved into position, then another. The picture was complete and perfect. This was Arizona.

It had been a long day of flying: from Las Vegas to Death Valley, California, the Mexican border and finally to Gila Bend, Arizona. I considered our progress. With the Pacific Coast reached, the country checked for leaks and Mexican air space overflown, we had done enough for one trip. It was time to go home.

But there was one last thing the Starduster and I had to do. On the way home I would pass through a small town in Colorado where the Rocky Mountain National Aerobatic Championships would be held. We couldn't miss that. My mind shifted from cross-country touring to barrel rolls and hammerheads.

The next morning I packed the luggage away with extra care and mounted the diagram of the Sportsman's Sequence on the instrument panel. So we flew north and east, rolling, snapping, looping and occasionally reversing with half a cuban, ever headed toward the pleasant prospect of familiar ground and old friends.

7/I Become a Competitor

For a change, the air was smooth as I slipped beneath the upside-down cake of the Denver Terminal Control Area. The once-difficult route was old stuff now. I put away the maps and relaxed, recalling the pleasant banter of the previous evening with Mike and Suzy Herbison at Colorado Springs, now 50 miles behind. They had surprised me with their intention to drive up and watch the weekend aerobatic competition at Longmont, a scant dozen miles from Boulder, my next stop. I planned to base my operations out of Boulder for the week in order to share Mike Ryer's foam-dome hangar and Sister Jess's gourmet cooking.

High over the Boulder Airport, an aircraft was going through an aerobatic routine, no doubt practicing for the upcoming contest. I patterned below, landed and wandered over to a shady spot to watch the show. I found myself standing next to Mike Ryer, who promptly gave me the benefit of his judgment on each maneuver.

The sequence I watched didn't look much like the stuff I had practiced, even though Mike said it was the same—the Sportsman's routine. My knowledge of contest-type aerobatics was so slim that I could not tell if the gent above was goofing his sequence, or if I had been practicing it all wrong. Mike did his best to explain the techniques, but without watching me perform, there was little he could do to help. Others were waiting their turn to practice, so I sat back and watched.

The pilot of the aircraft landed and walked over to join the group. His name was Robby Robinson, he was fifty-eight years old and a teacher at the local high school. He said that his aerobatics were lousy, but he loved every minute of it. I said that they looked okay to me, but that I was a poor one to judge, since I had the same problem. We watched several routines, especially Mike Ryer's complex sequence. Robby and I offered sage advice from our sophomoric stores of knowledge.

When Carl Bratfisch joined us, the conversation improved. He answered questions for both of us. His background gave him a bit of an edge, especially when it came to an appreciation of the precision of a maneuver. Carl was a colonel in the Air Force, based at Colorado Springs, but had just recently taken up serious aerobatics. The three of us, all "Sportsmen," would be competing against one another the next day. Robby and I figured that Carl would beat us both, leaving us to battle it out for last place.

Late in the afternoon Jay arrived. Having driven the 250 miles from Casper in a ground-born vehicle, she was weary and more than ready to retire to the Kellenbergers'.

For dinner, Jess fixed trout in almond butter sauce and served it with wild rice, June peas and pearl onions. We ate and we talked. Conversation began with recent developments within our families, and slowly turned to memories of the good old days. We visited until well past midnight.

Mike Ryer and I took off together at eight o'clock the next morning. Mike went on to the contest site, while I found a quiet spot to practice. While talking with the fellows, I realized that I had practiced two of the maneuvers in reverse. An hour later, the corrected moves began to feel natural, and I headed for Longmont.

There were a dozen aerobatic planes already parked on the ramp, and several more landed as I made my way to the registration trailer to pay my ten-dollar fee and have my papers checked. Proof of liability insurance was required, as well as membership in the EAA (Experimental Aviation Association) and the IAC (International Aerobatic Club). The airworthiness certificate and operations limitations were checked, and the plane and parachute inspected.

The inspectors were intrigued by my second seat belt. Such a belt is common, in fact required in all competing aircraft, but they had never seen one that utilized Velcro instead of the standard metal buckle.

"Are you positive this will take three negative g's?" one of the inspectors asked. I replied that we had lifted three grown men with the belt before it was installed.

"Well, we want to be sure—don't want the same thing happening to you that got Speed Holman."

He suddenly had my interest. "What exactly did happen to Holman?"

"His belt let go as he tried to pull up from an inverted dive and he fell halfway out of the cockpit. All he had to hang on to was the stick. Ever since his death, aerobatic pilots have worn a second seat belt," explained the inspector.

Since that conversation, I think about my boyhood hero every time I strap in.

The inspectors found an amazing amount of debris in the bellies of the various aircraft, each item capable of interfering with control movements and thus causing a fatal accident, but Second Sweetheart was clean. I had carried out my own inspection earlier, and in private embarrassment had retrieved a screwdriver that had been missing for three weeks!

I searched out my new friends, Carl and Robby. We looked over the competition. In all, twenty people had entered the Sportsman Contest. Among the group were two regional champions, a few airline pilots, two flight instructors and an airshow pilot. It would be rough company, especially for those of us competing for the first time.

One of the airline pilots, Jim McKinstry, a Western Airlines captain who ordinarily flew in a more advanced category, was competing in the Sportsman Event with a borrowed plane. He had wiped out his Pitts at a recent air show when debris lodged in his elevator control as he exited a loop. The plan destroyed itself as it impacted at a sharp angle on the runway. Pieces flew in all directions, but McKinstry crawled out unharmed, a tribute to the shoulder harness and sound aircraft design.

The planes on the ramp varied greatly in size and number of wings. There were high-winged T-Crafts, Bellanca Citabrias and Decathlons, and five kinds of biplanes, which included one Steen Skybolt, a dozen red Pitts and one wildly decorated Acroduster, a second cousin to the Starduster. Parked alongside Second Sweetheart was a light green plane of striking similarity. It was the two-place version called the Starduster Too, the design that caused all the confusion on my plane's center of gravity.

All the planes had one thing in common: On each instrument panel was a white envelope-sized card that displayed a strange assortment of figures called Aresti symbols. They are named for Count Aresti, the man who developed shorthand aerobatic notation. The circles, arrows, triangles, lines and dotted lines that crowded each card represented up to ten minutes' worth of aerobatics.

At the pilots' meeting, we learned the location of the aerobatic box, which was the same size as the one I had marked out at home. Corners and the center cross were laid out with white panels, and due to the altitude and its debilitating effect on lift, the top of the box was open. Sequences could begin as high as desired.

To eliminate the possibility of two planes in the box at once (it happens at almost every contest), we were to be held on the ground until the man above started his routine. Then we could climb up and enter as the man ahead vacated. Those with radios would get a double check on frequency 122.9.

It would be a four-category meet. All Sportsmen would fly once, with the scorers in the top third entitled to repeat. Those in the Intermediate category would all fly two sequences, the advanced group would fly three and the Unlimiteds would perform four times. The last two categories would have to fly an "unknown" sequence cooked up in great secrecy by the judges. All told, there were more than forty pilots flying nearly as many airplanes. It was to be a busy weekend.

It sounded like fun. Most of the pilots joked and fooled

around while they waited their turn. However, some appeared to be quite serious. "Doc" Carothers, dentist from Lincoln, Nebraska, took a small model plane from his kit and "flew" it through his unlimited sequences. His concentration was total, his eyes following the model as he moved it through an imaginary box. John Morrissey, an Air Force pilot from Kansas City, was even more intense. He closed his eyes and with hands flat like wings, walked through his sequence, mentally flying each maneuver.

I recognized the Sportsman's routine and thought perhaps I should join those doing the aerobatic dance. But on reflection I rejected the idea, figuring that the dance was for top hands only. It would be too embarrassing to be seen dancing the routine on the ground, only to later blow the whole thing in the air.

The Unlimiteds flew first. I stood by the P.A. announcer, Lloyd Wittenberg, another Western Airlines captain, who was also entered in the meet. His descriptions of the maneuvers were of great help, and he was happy to answer questions between routines. Mentally I polished my techniques: I would float over the top of each loop to make it round, and hold straight lines equal on either side of my rolls. If I came out crooked, I would hold the crook until I entered the next maneuver. "Never make an obvious correction," said Lloyd, "except in the interests of safety."

Jay and friends Mike and Suzy Herbison arrived before the Unlimiteds were finished. Mike asked about the competition, and Suzy told me I had to win. Jay wished me the best. I explained that it was all in fun, but there was a small seed of stage fright germinating in my midsection. I wanted to do well and not embarrass my supporters. I wanted to outscore Robby, and— dammit—I wanted to beat Carl Bratfisch too! I was caught up in the competition and getting serious, even to the extent of sneaking off to a secluded corner to walk through my sequence a few times.

The engine warmed as I sat on the ramp awaiting my turn. Overhead, Morrissey finished a flawless performance. Bratfisch was next. He started out well—much too well. I hoped he would blow a maneuver. Friendship goes only so far.

Now it's my turn. My stomach chases butterflies as I climb to 9,000. With the required wing-wag, I enter the box at 140 mph, level, barrel roll and level again (crisp and nice), then pull up to a

45-degree climb, hold it, then roll to inverted (not bad, but I wish I had a faster roll rate), now hold it, keep climbing inverted—a bit longer, since the speed is dropping—now ease back on the stick and come around, then back to level (not bad). Dive for speed—a quick look—150 mph, then a nice even slow roll—oops, keep the nose up (oh, oh, scooped it out the last quarter). Now up and over in a 5/8 loop, hold that 45-degree down line while inverted, then roll upright, hold the line and level up (perfect). I miss the outhouse and gravel pit markers of my own practice area, but am pleased to note on each down line that I am still centered over the big "X" in the center of the box. Next the loop—float her over—and pass through my prop wash at the bottom (beautiful). Now gain speed for a half loop and half roll (staggered out of that one). Now slow up for a 3/4-turn spin. Do it to the right. Here's where you had it reversed. Now straight down, out of the spin (not bad), pull up level, now straight up for a hammerhead. Look left to check wing on horizon, now wait, wait, as the speed dies on top, kick left rudder, put the stick in the corner—nothing happens— what's wrong? We're sliding back down. I lock up the stick and rudder and wait for the whip. Now we're pointed down (sure zeroed that maneuver). There goes my chance to beat Carl—and Robby too, most likely. Back to business (halfheartedly) 270-degree bank, hold the altitude now, straight through the box, back on the throttle, wait for 115 mph. Now—full throttle, and snap her. Dammit! I'm crooked—20 degrees off bank to the left! I straighten the wings smartly, then cuss myself for not flying out of the box on the slant. Wittenberg would be shaking his head at that mistake.

Back on the ground I quickly recounted my mistakes before anyone else could tell me about them. Carl listened carefully, nodding his head. Then just as I switched over to my good moves, he volunteered some pointers on my loop, spin and barrel roll, the ones I thought were perfect. Shot down by the Air Force!

Robby made me feel better. He forgot a couple of maneuvers and fell out of several more, but he enjoyed it. That was my problem. I took it seriously and forgot it was all supposed to be fun.

From all the talk, and from the routines I had observed, I figured on placing eighteenth or nineteenth out of twenty. When the scores were posted, I found I had placed seventh, behind Morrissey, 3588 points; McKinstry, 3370; Powell, 3329; Massegee, 3325; and Bratfisch, 3325. I scored 3066—in the top one-third—and was qualified for the fly-off!

My confidence returned and my ego reinflated. Damn—that wasn't bad for a guy that taught himself aerobatics. Besides that, mine was the only plane whose engine wouldn't run inverted. Maybe there was hope for future success in aerobatics. Now I was hooked—and I was *very* serious.

We adjourned to town for lunch. Mike brought a round of ale and toasted my success in tomorrow's fly-off. After a leisurely visit, we returned to the field to be met with instructions to roll the planes out and start up. Bad weather was forecast, and the fly-off had been moved up. We were due in the air right now!

I have a rule about drinking and flying. I like to keep them separated by at least twelve hours. There is an old adage, most often quoted in its aborted form: "Don't smoke within twelve hours, or drink within twenty feet of any airplane." It looked as if several of us were about to break the rule.

The contestant overhead was messing things up properly, falling out of his loop and flying out of the box. The next pilot crossed the deadline between the box and the crowd. That's a "no no," and brings an automatic zero score. There is only one other way to zero out, and that is to violate the 1,500-foot minimum height—the bottom of the box.

I missed Bratfisch's flight as I climbed to altitude, but I assumed he did well. Halfway through my routine, my mind went blank. I couldn't remember the next move. I wagged out of the box (it's legal), consulted my Aresti card and re-entered for the second half. Outside of the break the routine was good, except for the hammerhead, which was described as a semitorque roll by Announcer Wittenberg.

After landing, I filled up with gas. For me the competition was over. Rough air moved in as the last two contestants flew. You could see them bounce about. It wasn't a fair fly-off and those who suffered filed a verbal protest. Those who had done well wanted to let it stand. I didn't care, figuring I'd finish sixth or seventh anyway. Finally the decision came down. We would refly the fly-off on Sunday—weather permitting.

The scores on the disallowed flights were posted anyway. Unbelievably, I found that I had zeroed the loop! In fact, I plumb left it out. Strangely, several others, including Carl Bratfisch, had left out a move or two. And in his case it wasn't the beer, since Carl never touched the stuff. It seems that one must be mentally prepared if he is to do well.

Since I was now serious about the business of aerobatics, it was only reasonable to learn more about the method of scoring. Five judges evaluated each maneuver on a scale of 0 to 10. The high and low scores were thrown out, much like the scoring of Olympic diving. There was even a degree of difficulty, or "K" factor, calculated in afterwards. For example, 9 points on a maneuver with K 20 would be 180 points. I was surprised to find that the maneuver with the highest K factor was the hammerhead, the one I had thought I had mastered, but now consistently fouled up.

Planning to practice that maneuver, and burn off some excess gasoline at the same time, I rolled the plane out and began a walk-around inspection. By doing that I quickly learned another rule: No practicing was allowed once the meet started. In fact, the planes were virtually impounded for the duration of the contest. There was no way to drain the extra fuel, and at six pounds per gallon, that meant I would be hauling ninety unwanted pounds around. I wondered if the extra weight would help or hinder the hammerhead. The problem with that maneuver bothered me. Either I was doing something awfully wrong, or the plane was somehow at fault. I asked for advice, but no one had a solution to my problem.

The thunderstorms blew past during the night and the morning's bright blue skies and smooth air were welcome. The fly-off of the top seven in the Sportsman's category went quickly. My first maneuver was good. I was relaxed because I knew that my rank of seventh could not be worsened even if I zeroed the routine. However the 45-degree climbing roll did not go well. The plane was too heavy. After five maneuvers, I broke my sequence to climb for more altitude. Immediately, the radio man on the ground called for the next man to enter the box. I keyed in a frantic warning, "Stay out, stay out—I'm only half done!" There was no reply so I proceeded, eagle-eyed for an intruder. Surprisingly, the hammerhead went well, but I accidentally flew out of the end of the box (that cost 150 points) and finished up 300 feet below the minimum height. If the judges caught it, that could zero the whole flight.

Half an hour later the scores were posted. The judges had called me for "going out the bottom" and zeroed my flight. They were correct, of course, and I got what I deserved. However, seventh out of twenty was better than the last-place finish I had feared. Maybe I could have done better had I taken some dual instruction from an experienced competitor.

The two-hour flight home the next morning offered time to think and plan. There was a contest to be held on the Fourth of July at Council Bluffs, just across the river from Omaha. It would be bigger and tougher, but I was smarter now, and I would have almost a month to practice. If I could solve the hammerhead, I would be very competitive. Maybe if I climbed with a slight lean to the left, the plane would fall over better. I checked around for traffic and gave it a try. Usually I laid the left wing on the horizon as I headed up, but this time I lowered the wing so that it was centered on the horizon. Amazingly, we swung over and down under complete control. I tried again, this time checking the right wing's position on the horizon, and was shocked to see that it was also centered. Good grief! All my other "straight up lines" had been leaning to the right. No wonder the plane refused to fall left. Why hadn't other pilots seen it? Probably did, but were just being kind. How did I ever get such a bad habit?

Suddenly it became clear. I had flown a two-place Pitts a few months back. The wing position for straight up was on top of the horizon. When I climbed back into the Starduster, I carried the sight picture with me. I resolved to always check both right and left wings to ensure a vertical track. Well now! Competition was going to be a bit more interesting in the future.

Casper was 50 miles ahead. I kicked rudder and changed heading a bit to put us on a line with my private practice area, the one with the outhouse and gravel pit. I planned to be ready for Council Bluffs.

The month raced by, and the hammerheads became easy. Even the snap rolls, entered faster and with less elevator, became

100

predictable. My altitude conservation also improved. On a cool day, with minimum fuel, I could complete the sequence without a break to climb.

Rancher Steinle called frequently. He was relieved to see me practicing again, as he thought I'd done myself in somewhere. I listened to his criticism carefully, even though he professed ignorance concerning aerobatics. He was the only coach I had.

By the end of June, I was more than ready. I decided to leave for Council Bluffs a few days early, and perhaps practice along the way. I packed air mattress, tent and sleeping bag, plus a few cans of sardines and a handful of candy bars.

By the time the sun was high enough to warm the cockpit, we were halfway to Ogallala, Nebraska, riding a tail wind for all it was worth. By noon we had refueled at Grand Island and were on our way again. Just over an hour later, we put down at Council Bluffs. The contest was still two days off, but the ramp held a sprinkling of aerobatic craft. Apparently other pilots planned to do a bit of practicing too.

After registering, I flew on east to Perry, Iowa, for an overnight with relatives. (I have relatives and friends conveniently placed all over the country.) The next morning, I practiced the routine a few times in the quiet air above the runways at Perry, then flew on west, practicing along the way.

The ramp at Council Bluffs was crowded with aerobatic aircraft—twice the number that I had seen at Longmont. Our welcome was genuine. A 250-pound pig, which had been rotating over a charcoal fire since early morning, was carved up and served to us with beans, potato chips and beer. Tonight the practicing was over and the atmosphere was friendly and relaxed. Tomorrow it would get serious.

At eight the next morning, 67 pilots gathered for a briefing. Thirty of those pilots were entered in the Sportsman category. Everyone who beat me at Longmont was here to do it again. In addition, a national champion had shown up, along with a dozen more experienced competitors from all over the midwest. I could find just one other tyro among the group, my friendly nemesis, Carl Bratfisch.

My flight was scheduled near the end of the group. While waiting, I listened in on the judges' comments, trying to figure out how they wanted each maneuver done. I didn't see things the way they did—but then they weren't agreeing with each other either. Rancher Steinle's judgment looked pretty good by comparison. Several times during one flight I heard a judge on the left say, "Too steep," while the one on the right said, "A bit shallow." The judges differed widely on the barrel roll, with one judge giving tens as others scored threes and fours.

I was still uncertain as to just what they wanted to see, and how to fly the plane properly crooked so it would look right from their viewpoint. Flying for score was like painting a picture blindfolded, while five obstinate critics studied the work with magnifying glasses.

When it was my turn to fly, everything seemed to go just right—all except the hammerhead. I played it too safe, and skidded it over the top. When the scores were posted, Carl had 3355 points and I had 3204. We ranked 11th and 15th out of 30 and neither of us qualified for the fly-off. Eight pilots scored better than 3400 points, with Morrissey, the winner at Longmont, topping out with 3753.

As at Longmont, I was disappointed, yet at the same time encouraged. There was no question but that I could score in excess of 3600, given more experience with the business of flying for score.

Carl and I stretched out on our backs and watched the flights. The quality of pilotage in the more advanced categories was impressive. Some of the moves were unbelievable. Outside loops were common, and so were square and eight-sided loops. There were snaps going up, down and at the tops of loops. Unlimited pilots experienced up to 5 negative g's bottoming out of outside square loops, then felt hard positive g's in subsequent pull-ups. The abrupt change can let blood surge from the brain and put the pilot to "sleep," while the plane flies out of the box, wings aslant and uncontrolled. The "sleep" is rare and generally brief. Usually the pilot recovers before serious loss of altitude.

When done properly, aerobatics is an art form—an aerial ballet—a three-dimensional dance deserving of the finest symphonic accompaniment. Even when less than perfect, aerobatic flight is rare freedom and rarer privilege.

But for every privilege there is a price. After I left the

contest site, one of the contestants lost his life when his engine failed on climb out. He tried hard to save his plane, but stretched his glide too far. The aircraft stalled, spun to the ground and burned. The price was paid quickly.

8/To Saskatchewan

Flying Second Sweetheart to Canada would have been far easier had I remained ignorant of the special rules concerning experimental aircraft.

While I was building the plane, some kind soul had mentioned that homebuilts were not allowed to cross national borders without special permission. It took me three phone calls and four letters to locate the proper Canadian agency, and two more letters before I finally had a list of the required papers to be submitted. It was a good thing I started the procedure during the idle days of winter.

Three months later, a statement of authorization arrived along with a pamphlet containing rules pertaining to Canadian flying, and special rules for flight into the sparsely populated areas. Because my trip would take me one hundred miles or so past the "civilized" part of Saskatchewan, I was required to carry five pounds of dry food, cooking gear, matches, compass, knife and mosquito net. These items sounded fine, but the list went on: an ax weighing two and a half pounds or more, with a handle of twenty-eight inches or longer, thirty feet of snare wire, four trawls (whatever they were), two fishing lines with assorted hooks and a fishnet of not more than two-inch mesh.

Since my intention was to go fishing, I had two fishing rods along, packed in a special compartment in the rear fuselage, and a small kit of lures. I added one hatchet, some wire and the net portion of a landing net. The four trawls were left out since I could find no one who knew what they were. To my amazement, the list made no mention of flares, smoke bombs or signal mirror. These were standard equipment in N1NW.

My letter of authorization specifically prohibited aerobatic flight. I was disappointed, but soon learned that that particular rule was frequently bent.

My Canadian authorization, good for only seven days, began the day I returned from the contest at Council Bluffs, so that evening I checked the plane over, serviced the engine, charged the radio battery and stowed my gear. The equipment filled all the normal compartments, making it necessary to carry clothes and cameras in separate containers on the floorboards. The total load was a bit more than on the trip to the West Coast, but there would be no mountains to clear, and lift would improve when we found denser air in the low elevations of northern Saskatchewan.

At 7 A.M. I said good-bye to Jay and took off, headed north. An hour later we refueled at Sheridan, took off without delay and headed for Montana. Below our track, numerous coal-mining operations scarred the landscape and we flew over a number of ugly, unreclaimed pits.

As the U.S. border eased past below, I adapted my thinking to the Canadian rules of flight: Eastward flight was to be at odd thousands of feet in altitude, and westward was to be even thousands, both *without* the added 500 feet required in the United States. No VFR (visual flight rules) flights were to be made over clouds—from now on I had to stay underneath even the most sparsely scattered clouds. Radio frequency of 122.2 was to be monitored continuously "when practicable," according to the manual. With a limited life battery, "practicable" meant sparingly to me.

Presently we crossed the boundary of the control area surrounding Regina. I tuned the radio to 122.2, turned the volume up high and gave the tower a call. My five watts was apparently inadequate and I couldn't make contact. Five minutes later and ten miles closer, I tried again and received an answer immediately. After asking my altitude, Regina radio informed me of approaching traffic at 12 o'clock (head on), but 1,000 feet below. I was cautioned to maintain altitude.

I reported crossing the east-west highway just south of the airport as requested, and was promptly given clearance to land. On rollout, I inquired directions to Customs. The tower man obliged, then asked if the plane were aerobatic. I answered in the affirmative. After some hesitation, he asked if I did any aerobatics in the plane. I answered again in the affirmative, figuring he was just being friendly.

In short order, I went through Customs, filed my required flight plan to Prince Albert and was back at the plane looking for petrol. There was no tank truck available, so I gave the bloody windscrew a twirl, climbed in and taxied around the corner to the pump.

The oil was low and I asked for a quart of 50 weight. All they had was 100 grade. Quite a discussion ensued. Finally we all understood that 100 grade was Canadian for 50 weight American. With the windscreen freshly cleaned, one of the hands volunteered a twirl, and I proceeded to taxi out, proud of my new knowledge of the Canadian language.

When I called for clearance to the runway, the tower operator avoided answering, instead countering with more questions about aerobatics. I pulled on the parking brake and answered:

"Yes, the plane handles aerobatics nicely, and yes, I did a whole bunch just the other day."

"Would you put a show on for us?"

"I'd sure like to, but my authorization to enter the country prohibits aerobatics."

"Well, we can give you our permission."

"Can you override the prohibition?"

106

There was a long pause, then a deeper voice came over the radio: "We will override that."

So I staged a mini-airshow at busy Regina Airport, while two jetliners loaded passengers on the ramp below. I peeled down between runway 30 and the tower at 500 feet and 160 mph, put her on knife edge, held it, leveled, pulled up sharply and rolled. As I went over for the second time the cameras floated off the floorboards and I had to trap them against the instrument panel with one hand while completing my roll with the other. It was all a bit shaky, but as I flew away a voice on the radio murmured, "Beautiful, beautiful!"

On the ground at Prince Albert, the first three people I met asked me to put on an air show. The folks at Regina radio had probably passed the word up the line. I declined, refueled, filed my flight note for LaRonge, climbed in and took off. But the "schoolbus syndrome" prevailed. On takeoff I held the Sweetheart down for speed, then climbed almost vertically, half-hammerheaded and banked steeply to assume a course to LaRonge.

Signs of civilization dribbled away to a two-lane blacktop road that eventually changed to gravel. There were few cars, and I clung to the road like a child to a pacifier. It was lonely country. A forced landing away from the road would be disastrous, since it would be nearly impossible to move across the ground. Rivers, lakes and bogs interlaced with occasional ridgelike highlands called "eskers," forming a veritable maze.

We sailed along over a progression of quiet lakes, remaining always within gliding distance of the road. Soon Lac LaRonge filled the horizon. Some twenty by forty miles at the extremes, the lake was surrounded by trees and a mesh of connecting waterways. Its northern half was peppered with islands. Its southern half was open and dangerously inviting. From ground level you could not see the far shore.

LaRonge Town sat tight up against the western shore on a solid slab of granite. I could see several float planes taking off and landing, and several dozen more tied to the docks. The land port—a mile to the south—was quiet; even the radio service was shut down. After clearing the area for traffic, I circled overhead searching for the wind sock. Failing that, I took direction from the float planes and landed to the north.

The fishing camp, one of several located on the lakeshore, was operated by a young and friendly couple, Dave and Linda Longpre. Dave, a bush pilot until he bought the camp, had hopes of expanding the operation by adding a number of fly-in camps, and in the process getting back into active flying. In fact, he had a lake he wanted to check out, had arranged for the use of an 85-horse Cub on floats and asked if I would like to go along.

Shortly after breakfast the next morning, we loaded up the plane with one rod, three lures and gas to the brim of both tanks. Dave faced her into the wind and opened the throttle. Soon we were plowing water. Speed gathered slowly, and the wings took part of the load. Stick left and one float cleared the water, then with a sharp tug we were off and climbing. Dave was an accomplished pilot—probably had more time on floats, which Canadians call skis, than he had on wheels.

It was a pleasure to look out of the window and watch the floats pass over the wild landscape as we headed for the remote lake. The sight brought back pleasant memories of my first solo flight in a seaplane and I sank into a daydream as the miles rolled by.

My daydream ended as Dave eased the throttle and glided down to an effortless landing on the smooth waters of the lake.

Fishing was slow, and the first three trout threw the hook. We traded chores, paddling and casting. Fishing from a floatplane is awkward at best. Everything is in the way, and the footing is slippery.

The fish were there, which was what Dave wanted to know, so we taxied about the lake looking for a cabin site. Several sandy beaches offered ideal locations, but as weather began to move in discretion dictated a hasty departure.

The winds were squalling from the wrong direction, and after two abortive takeoffs we clawed our way into the air and headed home, dodging the low scud.

LaRonge was still socked in with fog the next morning and I wandered about the town, soaking up the frontier atmosphere. The single main street ran parallel to the shore, graveled in spots, but solid granite most of the way. Fishing camps and charter air services crowded the lake side of the road. Stores, cafés and a few residences stood opposite. Sewers and septic tanks were all but precluded by the solid rock foundation. Up until a few years ago there was only one flush toilet in town. Native Indians from hundreds of miles around made special trips just to flush it.

The whole town smelled of fish. For the sport fisherman, the smell was reassuring. When the boats returned in the evening, people gathered at the docks to view the catch and pick up a tip or two. Each boat carried a large washtup or a wooden box of equivalent size. In June and September the boats returned with overflowing boxes, happy fishermen and grinning, usually tooth-less, guides. But now, in July, the big fish were scarce and the boxes half empty.

The urge to go fishing—really fishing—returned as I watched a box holding a dozen four-pounders emptied in the cleaning house.

Dave had just the solution. His friend Ed Reine was camped nearby and looking for someone to go shares on a day's fishing. Ed, a retired Saskatchewan wheat farmer, was an avid fisherman, and a real character. We made a deal: Ed's outboard motor and knowledge of hot fishing spots would be matched by my boat rental and gasoline.

We headed out early the next morning, dodging reefs and rocks along the way. An hour later Ed took a couple of sights on nearby islands and said, "If I don't remember wrong, this is the spot."

We trolled with wire lines, and just as Ed was complaining that "they don't want to hook today," a nice one put a horseshoe bend in his stiff trolling rod. Soon we had a fine eight-pound lake trout thrashing in the fish box, and moments later a six-pounder joined it. We fished the rest of the day and headed home that evening with a respectable catch.

The weather was lousy the next morning. Fog reduced the world to a silent white hemisphere. The fish caught the day before were all filleted and frozen. Since his freezer at home was already full, Ed had donated his catch, and the twenty-odd pounds of pure, boneless fillets would fit nicely into one of Second Sweet-heart's unused wing compartments.

I stomped about town, touching base frequently with Dave and Linda Longpre to swap stories and listen to weather reports. The outlook was bad. When low ceilings gather over the shield

109

country they usually stay a while—up to a week, according to some of the long-time pilots. It was relaxing for the bush pilots, a time to rest and let the mechanics catch up. But time was running out for me. If I couldn't reach the United States in the next three days, my permit would expire.

The rains stopped in late afternoon, but the weather forecast remained discouraging. A new low-pressure system was to move in the next day and dominate the area for another week. There was, however, a chance for a few hours of marginal flying weather the next morning so I packed and made arrangements to pick up the fish at 6 A.M.

Next morning there was a noticeable thinning of the overcast as I walked to the local hotel for an early breakfast. An hour later, a patch of blue passed overhead as Dave helped me load up the Starduster, but soon it socked in again. We waited at the radio shack, looking west for lighter skies, as if wishing would make it so.

Perhaps the wishing did it. The ceiling rose to a thousand feet. I quickly filed my flight note and took off. The overcast lowered some as I approached the mild highlands halfway to Prince Albert, and I squeezed through with a hundred feet to spare. If it got worse, I would have to land on the road below, or head back. It did seem brighter ahead, so I took a chance and continued.

Twenty miles out of Prince Albert, the weather went below VFR minimums but it was too late to turn back. My gas would not reach. I called Prince Albert radio and explained my predicament. They could refuse permission to land, or they could bend the rules and let me sneak in.

Never underestimate the Canadians. They have a special way of handling such problems. I was asked to orbit a dozen miles north of the airport while they cleared the area of aircraft so that I would be the only blip on the nearby Saskatoon Radar. There was only one other plane in the air, and in a few moments, it was on the ground, and I was cleared for landing.

Now I had to find the airport. The hundred-foot ceilings and quarter-mile visibility made my task challenging. First I found the town of Prince Albert, then the river going east. Around the

110

first big bend, I turned left and came in the back door to the airport. No sweat!

Landing under minimums in a pinch was all right, but I would have to wait for 800-foot ceilings before departing. I drank coffee and loafed about the grounds until noon, when the men at Flight Service said another window was arriving that would let me get off for points south—at least to Saskatoon. I filed for Swift Current, 225 miles south, figuring to land at Saskatoon if the weather worsened.

We left as the window arrived, pointing upstream and south-southwest along the Saskatchewan River. Soon the skies brightened. Five large white birds with black wingtips appeared ahead. As we closed, their large yellow bills revealed them to be pelicans. We were almost even with their formation when the left wingman noticed us and they evacuated in unison, diving steeply.

Saskatoon showed clearly a point or so to starboard. Like most Saskatchewan cities, it looked bright and clean, even under dark skies. I reported my progress to Saskatoon radio, receiving a satisfactory weather report and continued on course for Swift Current.

A visit to the Swift Current Flight Service reminded me that since it was Sunday, U.S. Customs would be closed and there would be a twenty-five-dollar fee to open the office at Glasgow, Montana. As there was too little time to make it all the way home and I had to overnight somewhere, I decided it might as well be in Swift Current. I had one day left to reach the U.S. without violating my permit.

During the night, the edge of the overcast drifted south instead of east as expected. I hurried to the airport, passing up breakfast, to get off as quickly as possible. It was still bright to the south, but closing down rapidly from the north. Some of the scud looked familiar.

The ceiling went below minimum as I taxied out to the end of the runway. I had to receive clearance before takeoff. Swift Current Flight Service knew that I was headed for the brighter skies to the south, and to delay me now would hold me up several days. They cleared me in spite of the low ceiling. Nice folks, these Canadians.

For fifty miles we dodged clouds and power lines. Suddenly it was clear again and we rose to a comfortable altitude to cross the invisible line, the 49th Parallel, that separates those who say "troot" from those who say "trout."

The homing instinct came on strong as the Big Horn Mountains showed a faint line ahead. Individual peaks stood out as we approached Sheridan on the Wyoming border. For a change the wind was calm, but the temperature was nearly 100 degrees. The full tanks and the extra weight of the fish packed in the wing made the takeoff from Sheridan Airport less than spectacular. We staggered out and climbed slowly into cooler, smoother air.

There is time aplenty to dream when the air is smooth and the course is known. Each sight below sparks a different thought.

This was the favorite country of the legendary mountain man Jim Bridger some 100 years ago. "Old Gabe," as they called him, used to call the Big Horns his "Shining Mountains," and he would tell lies about "seein' clear through 'em." He claimed they "magnified rock chucks to look big as elk" and that all the mountains in the territory "was jes' little hills" when he got there, and that they had "growed some since."

Fifty miles ahead, Casper Mountain showed its rounded outline. We were nearly home. I studied the mountain carefully. It didn't look one whit bigger than the day we left. I had kind of hoped it might have "growed some since."

9/A Gathering of Egos

The grand gathering at Oshkosh—the yearly bash of the Experimental Aircraft Association—was scheduled for the last week in August. That gave me ten days to relax, inspect and tend to Second Sweetheart's minor ailments, as well as gather maps and lay out the longest trip of the summer.

Oshkosh was a mere 900 miles away, but it would only be an extended stop on the way to the East Coast. Once I reached the Atlantic shore, my border-to-border and coast-to-coast goals would have been accomplished.

It took eleven sectional charts to cover the proposed route. I planned to visit Park Rapids, Minnesota; Oshkosh, Wisconsin; Chicago, Illinois; Goochland, Virginia; Kitty Hawk, North Carolina; and Muscatine, Iowa.

The trip would last about two weeks, requiring an amount of gear, mostly clothing, that overtaxed the plane's capacity. I sacrificed the chute and replaced it with two changes of clothing, then wrapped up three more changes to be mailed ahead to Oshkosh. It was the wrong season to leave cool Wyoming and head for hotter and more humid areas. I expected to sweat a lot.

The sun rode low on the horizon as we headed east, looking for the dark bulge of the Black Hills. They rose and sharpened on schedule. We passed over the town of Custer and skirted the southern end of the mountains. Mount Rushmore, a few miles to the north, was hidden under torrents of rain. Rapid City, visible over the nose, was momentarily free of precipitation. We gassed up quickly and were off again. The best tailwind was at 9,600 feet, so we rose to ride with the helping wind and enjoy the cooler air. To minimize the effect of the descent to Aberdeen's elevation of 1,300 feet, I began a gradual letdown 80 miles out. We landed under sunny skies dotted with a fresh crop of budding cumulus clouds.

North and east of Aberdeen, we nicked a corner of North Dakota, crossed the north-flowing Red River and entered the State of Minnesota. The air felt cooler immediately. The clouds were older here, sporting flat bottoms and slow-boiling tops.

The landscape below changed from crops and deciduous trees to water and pines. I put the maps away and enjoyed the familiar outlines of the lakes passing below.

Mature thunderstorms rose before us and we threaded our way through the deep canyons of space between them, watching lightning shoot bright jagged lines from the virga that bottomed each storm cell. Sounds of thunder were lost in the roar of the engine, and the view from the cockpit reminded me of a scene from an old silent movie.

The air began to roughen. Gratefully we sloped down over the trees and slipped sharply to the grass runway at Bill Riedesel's little airport south of Park Rapids, Minnesota. We had traveled 650 miles in five hours—what a freedom machine!

Bill stood by the hangar, all smiles as I taxied up. His help in overhauling the engine two years earlier gave him a great deal of satisfaction. He ran his hands over the curves of the Starduster, happy in the knowledge that I had built the plane with skills learned at his direction.

Two of Bill's friends arrived and moved around the plane passing out compliments. One of the men, a Starduster Too

114

builder, paid the ultimate compliment by claiming that he was going straight home to take a piss-elm branch to his half-built plane. The second gentleman was more concerned with performance.

"How quickly does she get off?"

"I don't really know—probably six, eight hundred feet at this altitude."

He disagreed and offered to bet, both of us knowing that all he wanted was to see the plane fly.

We didn't measure it, but with the luggage out and a firm breeze on the nose, she got off in grand fashion. I hung her on max climb at 80 per, then put on an impromptu airshow. We looped and rolled, hammerheaded and snapped, slipped and finally landed.

At eight the next morning, I climbed into the cockpit, stuffed full of Ginny Riedesel's country-style breakfast. Once airborne, I picked out a lake on the desired track ahead, took a compass reading and relaxed, letting the Sweetheart handle the business of flying while I took in the sights. Smoke rose from a sawmill, bent west, rose some more, then leaned hard east. I matched altitude with the east leg and watched the ground-speed climb.

Just south of Duluth, and barely short of Wisconsin, my way was blocked by a solid bank of fog. I couldn't fly over it—the gas tank would probably go dry before I found a hole—so I tried to go under and the world dissolved in white, forcing me into an uncomfortably low 180.

I landed at the nearest airport, a lonely grass strip whose faded sign read "Sandstone Municipal Airport—phone for gas or taxi." Inside the adjacent shack, I sat down on a well-chewed overstuffed chair, and waited for the fog to lift. A note was pinned to the space heater that read, "Don't light fire—bird's nest in smoke pipe."

An hour later, I fired up the plane and went up for a look. The path was still blocked. Another hour, another try, and this time the fog was breaking up into patches. We headed east, zigzagging to remain over open ground. At Rice Lake, Wisconsin, the fog closed in again, but we needed to land there for gas anyway.

After refueling at Rice Lake we headed southeast. The land beneath us changed from lakes to meadow, then to mixed crop and dairyland. We ran into head winds and our speed suffered. It took nearly two hours to cover the 150 miles to Waupaca.

A twin-engined aircraft was departing Waupaca as we entered the pattern. I tuned in Unicom frequency just in time to hear the pilot of the twin ask: "Who's up there in that little biplane?"

"It's me, Norm Weis, from Casper, Wyoming."

"Sorry I missed you," came the reply.

Waupaca was delightful. Nice pilots' lounge, hot coffee, new nylon rope tie-downs (at no charge) and a café across the street. Oshkosh was a twenty-minute hop away, so I could pop in early the next morning and avoid the convention traffic.

I pitched my tent alongside Second Sweetheart's right wing, inflated the air mattress and fluffed up the sleeping bag. The seat and back cushions made an excellent pillow. I laid out canteen, flashlight and reading material, locked the camera in the baggage compartment and retired to the shade of a large cottonwood tree across the street. My beer was cold and the trunk of the tree met my back in all the right places. A mild breeze sprang up as the sky darkened. It would be a good night for sleeping.

The sun was well over the horizon by the time I rolled and stowed away the gear. The engine started on the first try, and I was off to see the elephant—the grand extravaganza called Oshkosh.

Traffic was light—only a dozen planes flew the pattern over Oshkosh. Lacking the proper frequency, I joined the no-radio group and landed the first go 'round.

A pickup truck full of ground handlers directed me to a parking spot. I dug out the tie-down stakes and laboriously screwed them into the hard ground, then tied the plane's wings and tail securely.

At the registration booth I filled out the forms that entered Second Sweetheart in the judging for the best homebuilt. I signed a statement attesting to the fact that I had done at least 50 percent of the building (actually 98 percent), then paid my fees and headed back to unload the plane.

Planes were everywhere—landing, departing, forming up in display lines, filling camping spots, settling in for the week-long air show. Within a few days there would be more than 420 home-builts, 150 antiques, 140 war birds, two dozen rotor-craft and a handful of creations that defied classification. In all, there would be 1,260 on display, and 300,000 people would view them. They arrived by car and by plane, and they stayed at the campground, the motels, or the university dorms. The 50,000 citizens of Oshkosh were overwhelmed by the influx.

The entire west side of the airport was filled with planes. Thousands of store-bought craft crowded the parking areas and created a havoc in the air that challenged the traffic controllers. More than 70,000 arrivals and departures could be expected during the week, making Oshkosh temporarily the busiest airport in the world. Airline pilots had been known to pass up their scheduled stops at Oshkosh because of the confusion. Planes formed long lines in the air awaiting their turn to land. Controllers had no time for such niceties as numbers and letters. It was, "red low-winger, you're next—stretch your glide and land at the far end; yellow bipe, pour it on, stay close to the red low-wing; blue Cessna, you're long, go around; silver Beech, put it down now, right now, then get off the runway to the left! Come on folks, close it up. Red Cessna, stay right and put it on the numbers. BLUE BEECH, GET OFF THAT RUNWAY! Everyone, taxi on the grass only."

And on it would go for an entire week. And that was just the runway for store-bought aircraft. A separate runway was reserved for experimentals and such. At times that runway was even busier.

I wandered about, getting into the spirit of things. The letters E.A.A. were everywhere: on signs, on every airplane, on caps and patch-covered jackets. I saw them on pins and T-shirts, even earrings and coffee cups, all offered for sale. Two-dollar film was selling for $3.95, and there were fees to camp, fees to enter the ground, fees to enter the display area and, of course, a fee to join the Experimental Aircraft Association. I began to resent the fact that I had to pay a fee to display a plane that others had to pay a fee to see.

Yet, the E.A.A. is a nonprofit organization. Loyalty within

the group is fantastic. I seemed to be the only one possessing doubts. My hesitant questions were met with amazement. No one, it seemed, had ever heard a disparaging word used in connection with the E.A.A. Apparently I was out of step.

For would-be airplane builders, the show was a grand place to gather vital information. For tourists, it was a chance to see lots of planes. For some, it was a place to let the kids run loose. For others, it was a place to learn a skill; even take part in some construction at one of the do-it-yourself workshops. For the businessfolk, it was a place to hawk their wares.

Out on the ramp numerous aircraft were on display, with owners or agents on hand to dispense information as to cost of construction, performance and the availability of plans. Selling plans is a big business. Of course, it's nearly impossible to design your own craft, and plans are vital and well worth the money— especially if they represent a craft designed by an aeronautical engineer. But few people realize that 1,000 sets of $150 plans add up to $150,000, and that's big business. Only one buyer in sixty ever completes his plane, so the sale of plans is a matter of selling dreams, and I can't knock that—for dreams are rare at any price.

After dark, I caught a bus for town and settled into my dorm room at the university. It was sweltering. At midnight it was still hot and sleep was impossible. While those lucky Southerners slept comfortably, the group from cooler places sat in the lobby, watched television and sweated.

More homebuilt craft arrived the next morning, and the competition escalated. I thought the Sweetheart was the finest homebuilt on display until a wildly painted Pitts trundled in. Its finish was like a mirror. The three colors of paint met so smoothly that the joints defied detection, even by fingertip.

Down the line, a trio of BD4s parked and new ropes were strung along stanchions. One proud owner stretched nearly 100 feet of white plastic chain about his plane, set up large information easels and relaxed on a matching white chaise lounge. His airplane was flawless—metallic paint job in subdued tones of green; dark Plexiglas, super upholstery, and desert scenes airbrushed neatly along the center lines of the fuselage and wheel pants.

Before all the contesting aircraft had arrived, I had reduced my rank from a hopeful first or second, to twelfth or below—and they only went three or four deep on the prizes. However, there was always an award for the best Starduster, and there I thought I had a chance, although seven or eight Stardusters had already arrived.

Just then another Starduster showed up, sporting a military paint job that rivaled mine in workmanship, and I became instantly jealous. I wandered over to visit with the owner. He seemed a decent sort and we small-talked like a couple of banty roosters. But our pleasant words were quite the opposite of our thoughts.

Down the line, the builders of two blue and yellow biplanes were going through the same routine. Their discussion heated up over the question of cruise speeds, then cooled as they watched a third even classier blue and yellow biplane taxi up with a young woman at the controls. It was a gathering of egos (and mine was second to none).

Of the twenty or so biplanes, I figured the Sweetheart was the finest, but I was looking through owner's eyes. A light green Starduster Too came close and I'm sure the owner eyed my plane similarly, but there was no rivalry here, for old Doug Pfundheller, a Norwegian, was very friendly. His family was camped a few blocks away in the drive-in campground and we got along famously. Norwegian hospitality is exceptional.

Doug hung a sign on his plane that said, "Please do not touch or caress," and it worked. However, we both stayed close to our planes. The hordes of visitors, although mostly well mannered, were known to flop ailerons, climb in cockpits, bump and bend elevators and, worst of all, lean over to look into the cockpit while babes in arms kicked hell out of the fabric. If it wasn't babies, it was neck-strapped cameras that banged and rebounded. We all developed baby rash and camera dents. Now I understood why so many owners had brought rope and stanchions along.

At times I turned my back on my worries over tourist damage and walked over to the workshop area to listen to a particularly interesting seminar, or take part in a workshop. But always I returned quickly to take care of the plane. Then too, I didn't want to miss the judging team as it made the rounds. Some of the owners stuck around until dark, hoping to add a swaying word or two. We all assumed that the judges—probably a team of half a dozen experts—would look each plane over carefully: top, bottom, inside, outside, even lift the cowl.

There was much discussion about the great number of homebuilts that had actually been built by professionals. One past winner had claimed his 50 percent, but it turned out he had hired his welding, bought his fittings, had a friend build the ribs, hired a professional to cover the plane, and farmed out the upholstery and paint job. He did fly it to the contest. I began to understand how the unbelievable paint jobs and upholstery I had seen on some of the "top twelve" had been achieved.

Thousands of visitors wandered through the display area each day. Most of them asked the same questions: "How much did the plane cost? Do you really fly it? Did you fly it here from Casper? How many hours did it take?" And they oohed and ahed in admiration over such a long trip, as if each hour were perilous.

The job of plane tending became easier when I blew up the air mattress and stretched it under the shade of the right wing. I lay there for hours, fielding questions, occasionally reading and always hearing the click of cameras held by people who thought me a comical sight.

The week long fly-in is a good experience for the flying buff, the sightseer and the would-be homebuilder. I envied them as I stood by the plane, my freedom restricted and opportunities to look and learn severely limited. If I had made an earlier visit as an observer, my Oshkosh experience would have been far more pleasant. It's a mistake to display a plane on the first trip.

Air shows were held at the end of each day, and they were the best feature of the convention. Performers vied for a chance to show their skills, and they did it for free several hours a day. For the entire week, the air shows went on—and seldom was an act repeated. Most of the acts were outstanding, although a few of them were quite similar to the type of show that I had put on for the college faculty. Perhaps I wasn't so far from professional quality air-show work as I had thought. One performer made his Waco biplane stand on its tail briefly. It was a quirk of the plane that he had discovered quite by accident. I resolved to experiment with the Starduster and see if it had any unusual moves within its makeup. Perhaps I could invent a new maneuver.

Wednesday rolled around without any sign of the judges. Worse, my clean clothes had not come. Rainy weather arrived, but that was welcome. It would hold down the visitors and temper the heat.

Between rain showers, a young pilot at the south end of the field had been making short flights in his powered, tailless glider. He would fire up the engine, hoist the rig and run into the wind, retracting his feet as flying speed as obtained, then climb laboriously for altitude. I watched him execute steeper and steeper wingovers, marveling at the glider's stability. Every tailless model airplane I had ever built flew only briefly before spinning like a rotating reel in an old push-mower.

A few flights later, the pilot overdid his aerobatics and flipped over on his back. Immediately the wings began to roll over like the reel I had been thinking about. He fell as he rolled, and passed behind a large hangar, still rolling. I hurried over to find the pilot and machine both intact. On the way down he had been shifting his weight back and forth to no effect, but after shutting off the power and shifting weight once more, the plane stabilized a few feet over the ground. E.A.A. officials were on hand, as well as an ambulance or two, and the pilot was grounded for the duration of the meet.

Skies cleared the next day and the crowds increased. Long lines formed for every necessity. I stood in line for coffee, hot dogs, a drink at the fountain and a chance to use the outhouse. Someone deep in one of the lines voiced the sentiment: "Oshkosh is a nice place to live, but I wouldn't want to visit."

Six of us missed the bus to the airport the next morning, so we chipped in for a cab. As we neared the airport, we saw an approaching plane strike the ground and flip over. Although we were still several blocks from the terminal, we could clearly see two people scramble from the wreckage and run, then stop and stare in horror as spilled fuel ignited the plane, which flared brightly. Later we learned that the plane had carried three people, and sadly, one of them did not get out in time.

It surprised me that there weren't more accidents, especially on the runway reserved for the experimentals. The "fly-by" pattern above the runway was always crowded. Sometimes thirty or forty aircraft made endless circles, some landing, some taking off to enter the circuit. To fly the circuit, pilots were required to attend one of the many briefings held each day. The briefings were put on by volunteer FAA people, and if it wasn't such serious business, the proceedings would have been hilarious.

The thrust of each briefing was to the effect that certain hours were for slow planes, other hours for those of medium speed and still others for fast planes. There would be NO racing, NO abrupt pullups, and NO turns below 200 feet. All takeoffs and landings would be handled by the signalmen on the runway. After stating wind velocity and direction of flight on the circuit the volunteers handed each pilot a colored card of a certain shape as proof of attendance, and permission to fly the circuit.

But as soon as pilots climbed into their planes, the rules seemed to be forgotten. As if by common consent, most pilots made zooming climbs and showy low-level approaches. And races—there were lots of informal races every day. The colored cards given out at briefing were seldom asked for at the runway, and slow, medium and fast aircraft were frequently in the pattern together.

The word was out. The judging was finished! The winners would be announced later that day. No one along the biplane lines had seen the judges, but a pilot from the next row said they had driven by one day in the rain, rolled down the car windows and looked—at some planes, he claimed, they hadn't even stopped the car! Well, none of us expected to be in the running for the sweepstakes, but there was still the prize for the best biplane.

Then the ax fell! The donor for the biplane trophy hadn't come through. That meant all our waxing and polishing, waiting and hoping, had been in vain.

The biplane pilots propped up their crippled egos and turned their attentions to the trip home. For me it was easy. The best part of my trip was still ahead and I was looking forward to more adventures with Second Sweetheart on my trip to the Coast.

10/Kitty Hawk the Hard Way

It was a relief to be alone and free of crowds. We were a mile above the ground, cruising north, paralleling the spur of Lake Michigan called Green Bay. Plans to head for Chicago, then southeast toward Kitty Hawk, had been changed by the persistent rain-filled low-pressure system that occupied southern Wisconsin and most of Illinois and Ohio. I had always wanted to visit Mackinac Island (they call it "Mackinaw"), and the weather was an easy excuse.

The entire island was an historic landmark. Located a scant fifty miles from the Canadian border, it commanded the strait between Lakes Huron and Michigan. Although no cars were allowed on the island, access by air was permitted. It would be a nice place to wind down after suffering the crowds of Oshkosh.

After landing on the single runway and tying the Starduster down, I began the one-mile walk to town. I hadn't gone far before I was overtaken by a stoutly wheeled dray, pulled by a team of horses. I bummed a ride on the tailgate, dangled my feet and enjoyed the view. The road was deeply shaded in tall pines whose needles muffled the clop of the horses' hooves. It was marvelously quiet.

Main Street ran parallel to the south shore of the island, and was faced on both sides with small shops and cafés. The side streets of town were steep and it was common to see a string of bicycles catching free uphill rides behind horse-drawn vehicles.

I climbed to the ramparts of Fort Mackinac, high on a promontory at the east edge of town. The Fort is intact and worth the two-dollar entrance fee for a chance to wander about the halls and to view the Straits from its high parapets.

On the opposite side of the town, the impressive Grand Hotel caught my eye and I went to have a look at its old-time elegance. Built in 1878, with fancy woods and loving care, the building has remained in marvelous repair and full working order. More than 800 feet long, and fronted all the way with a column-supported three-story porch, the magnificent structure dominates the island's west overlook.

Just inside the main entrance was a sign, "Ties and coats are required after 6 P.M." Feeling the need of a little class but having no coat and tie, I dined out in the finest place in town that did not require them, then took a one-horse taxi to the airport. I pitched my tent beside Second Sweetheart as the sun spread color over the western sky. With flashlight and book, I read myself to sleep—the first good sleep in a week.

At Jackson, Michigan, I learned that a low-pressure area covered most of the Appalachians, and that Hurricane Belle on the coast was holding the weather system in place. I decided to head south and skirt the west edge of the overcast.

Marysville, Ohio, was as far as I could go. I was stuck there for three days while Hurricane Belle made a slow curve to the northeast, then finally headed out to sea.

The air was clear and the sky was cloudless as we departed Marysville. A few miles south, smog covered the city of Chillicothe like a poisonous blanket. Beyond, the sky turned dirty brown and plumes of red and black smoke compounded the problem. At Ashland, the visibility dropped to two miles, requiring special radar clearance and a five-minute wait in order to land.

The poor visibility had me a bit spooked, and I sought advice concerning the best passage through the Appalachians. "Just head up the canyon," the man said. "Keep going as long as you can see to the next bend. That's the way we all do it. Of course, if you had the instruments, you'd be better off on top."

The overcast sat like a lid on the canyon rim, and we flew the open notch, following the bends out of necessity. It was nervous work, and I disliked it intensely. My hand ached from gripping the stick, and time crawled.

My disgust turned to stage-one fear when a half-completed bridge loomed out of the mist half a mile ahead. Construction work meant guy wires, and that meant I had to go over, not under, even if the space below looked ample. I climbed to test the ceiling, figuring on a quick hammerhead turn if things went bad. The clouds rode 100 feet above the rim. I turned south, crowded between the clouds and the town of Fayetteville below, and white-knuckled my way through a long curve back to the relative safety of the canyon, carefully following our slow progress on the map.

At Hinton, we turned south, and with great relief followed the flat eastern shore of Bluestone Lake. Then, with lifting ceilings, we overflew the narrows at Pearisburg and took a straight line for Roanoke, Virginia.

The blacktop ramp at Roanoke felt particularly solid and reassuring. I dawdled over several cups of coffee before calling Dan and Ruth Steck, old friends now living in Goochland, Virginia. We agreed to meet in Charlottesville, 100 miles northwest of Roanoke and forty-five minutes away over comfortable terrain.

Riding in an automobile was a welcome change. I spent the evening and the next day touring the various construction projects Dan had going, and generally relaxing, waiting for the smog to clear. Dan and Ruth finally convinced me that the haze was normal, so I made plans to fly to Kitty Hawk the next day. Dan located a small private strip just north of Goochland, and secured permission for me to land on my return from the Coast.

The smog enclosed us as we climbed out of Charlottesville. It was a thin brown version of the white stuff I had encountered over Los Angeles and formed a bowl around the plane, growing and shrinking, but always affording a few miles of visibility. We climbed, and the sky above became blue, but the ground visible below closed down like the diaphragm of a camera. We flew past Richmond, dropped in at Chesterfield County Airport for fuel, then headed southeast, carefully tracking progress on the map while keeping an eye on the bottom of the bowl.

There is one advantage to smog flying. Other aircraft stand out as black silhouettes, with no chance to hide in the camouflage of mottled ground. The possibility of a midair collision is minimized.

At Suffolk I filled up for the 240-mile round-trip flight to Kitty Hawk. The Great Dismal Swamp occupied the land under a short, straight-line course. Common sense dictated a track south along the railroad, then down the wide Chowan River and east along the edge of Albermarle Sound to the long cape that stood off the coast. Detours around restricted areas and the Coast Guard Port at Elizabeth City added to the distance.

With just over half a tank of gas remaining, I caught sight of the dunes of Kitty Hawk below. The skies at the coastline were a surprising blue, well speckled with small puffs of cumulus. The bright sunlight flashed off the choppy waters of the Atlantic while the onshore breeze held the smog at bay.

I wheeled overhead, reconstructing the path of the Wrights' first flight, then dropped down and rolled the wheels briefly on the small strip adjacent to the monument.

There was no time to dawdle. The fuel supply was almost half gone. With throttle retarded and mixture lean, we began the slow trip back.

Prior to the trip, I had done a bit of reading about the Wright Brothers. Aviation texts generally agree that the two men have been badly served by historians. Their engineering skills were phenomenal. Not only did they develop a controllable flying platform, but also the engine to match, along with the first airfoil-shaped propeller. Their propellers were more than 70 percent efficient. Sixty years later, propeller efficiency had been boosted to only 85 percent.

But most of all, they were persistent. Wilbur wrote to Octave Chanute on May 13, 1900: "For some years I have been affected with the belief that flight is possible to man. My disease

126

has increased in severity and I feel that it will cost me an increased amount of money, if not my life."

On completion of the brothers' first successful glider flight, Wilbur wrote his father, Bishop Milton Wright: ". . . The man who wishes to keep at the problem long enough to really learn anything positively must not take dangerous risks. Carelessness and over-confidence are usually more dangerous than deliberately accepted risks."

One can but envy their industry and their genius. Perhaps it would not be pleasant to live a life filled with such determination, but if I could have controlled my own ancestry, I would like to have been one part Wilbur, one part Orville, two parts Will Rogers, two parts Lindbergh, three parts Speed Holman, plus a dash of Wrong Way Corrigan, the fellow who took off from New York alone in an old Curtis Robin headed for Los Angeles, but ended up flying the Atlantic—quite on purpose. My wish carries no dissatisfaction with my lot. Quite the contrary, as I consider it miraculous that I was born in the twentieth century. Of the thousands of generations that trod the ground and watched the birds, my turn came when man first took to the air!

Fuel was bouncing on the empty mark as the Sweetheart's wheels rolled to a stop on Suffolk's wide runways, once used by Billy Mitchell as short field takeoff training for the B-25s that raided Tokyo early in the war.

Nearing Goochland, I spotted Dan's car pulling into the outskirts of the small village. It was air-show time. I passed by his vehicle at eye level and legal distance, climbed to comfortable altitude and ran through a rapid sequence of loops, hammerheads and cubans, then headed for the private strip a few miles north.

Two days later, after Dan, Ruth and I had discussed and solved all the world's problems, I took off again, this time headed home. The reliable smog, which Dan had insisted was purely natural, seemed to keep pace as we flew west-southwest, planning on a gas stop at Lynchburg.

The Clinch Mountains paralleled our track as we searched for an easy pass through the Appalachians. The map indicated a reasonable passage from Norton to Cumberland, but 60 miles further, the gap at Middlesboro looked even better. Strangely, the map showed the southernmost passage to be "Cumberland Gap," well removed from the town of the same name.

Tree-covered mountains rose sharply and crowded both wings as we entered the gap. Like the playful ax mark of some forgotten giant, it formed an open wedge, momentarily breaking the steady march of the Cumberland Range. Beyond, the land gentled to rounded hills, bounced down and leveled.

We landed at a place called London. Sectional charts made light of state lines, and I was not at all sure just where I was. I asked the young man handling the gas hose, and received a look of pure disgust, along with a grudging, "Kentucky." The wall map in the office showed that after leaving Virginia, I had clipped a corner of North Carolina, entered Tennessee, then passed into Kentucky at the Gap.

At Seymour, I played it cool and consulted the wall map first. Indiana! The name had a pleasant, friendly ring. There was plenty of room in the big hangar, and sure, I could sleep with the plane if I liked. The man even smiled in understanding. I'm sure he figured I wanted to be with the plane to ensure its protection, when in reality my finances had reached the point where I had to choose between soft beds and gasoline. Then again, maybe he had me properly figured, since he gave me a ride to town and pointed out his favorite hamburger joint.

Thunderstorms struck at 2 A.M. I lay awake, comfortable on my air mattress, head resting against the wheel pant, enjoying the play of lightning, listening for the trailing thunder. The broad doors of the hangar stood wide open, but we were tucked well back, safe from wind and rain. Soon thunder and lightning came as one, and the storm stood overhead, delivering rain, then hail, then rain again. The thunderstorms marched all night, but in the morning the world was beautiful.

Puffy newborn cumulus clouds rose slowly to begin their daily growth. We flew below them, then among them, and soon bested their modest heights. The sky was a delirious blue and the clouds tumbled by as we chased the wind westward.

My older brother, Homer, lived just 400 miles ahead at a place called Muscatine, Iowa. I planned to be there in three hours enjoying family talk, eating a forepromised dinner of catfish and

128

corn on the cob. As I mentioned before, I had family scattered about the country in the most strategic places.

On arrival, I learned that the corn was on hand, but the fish had yet to be caught. Homer claimed he had them all staked out in his favorite fishing hole in the middle of the Mississippi River but the fish failed to favor his rig. We ate my catfish and his wife Mary's corn on the cob.

Bad weather followed good, and it was two days before Second Sweetheart cleared ground. We flew northwest, making gas stops at Marshalltown and Forest City, Iowa. Inquiries concerning runway conditions at Lake Mills, Iowa, brought strong caution concerning wet, muddy runways at that town's small airstrip.

I had taught physics at Lake Mills High School thirty-five years earlier, and wanted badly to revisit. One of the students at that school was responsible for my first flying lesson. He challenged a statement I had made concerning the theory of flight and backed up his knowledge by telling the class he had just flown an airplane all by himself!

I set out to equal his credibility, and in the process met a most interesting character, Eldon Hagen. He owned a little yellow and orange high-wing tandem two-place Aeronca 7AC, affectionately referred to as the "air knocker," and he charged seven bucks dual and five solo. His airfield consisted of a 40-acre grass patch with one T hangar, a tiny shack and a gas pump. The longest runway was 1,600 feet, with a fence at both ends. All in all, it was a perfect place to learn to fly.

Eldon was a practical joker. If I forgot my seat belt, he could hardly wait to get enough altitude to pop the stick and float me to the ceiling. I forgot often, and each time the trip to the skylight carried more force. Once I thought landings had been mastered, Eldon would occasionally bring on a king-sized bounce or two with the same wicked shove on the stick. Those bounces helped me to save the Cub from crashing into the junk pile a few years later.

In the winter, when wheels were replaced with skis, the field seemed to shrink as the packed snow changed to ice. My frantic use of wheel brakes, which had no effect at all on skis, brought old Eldon to fits of laughter. But he was watching—if he was certain a stop could not be made short of the fence, he would jam the throttle forward and suggest that I take off and try again.

Eldon showed me my first loop and let me try a few. Of course we tried a snap or two. That was merely a spin turned sideways, and spins had already been covered—they were required for a license back then. The brief taste of aerobatics he gave me whetted my appetite for more and eventually led me to Second Sweetheart.

The old 40-acre airfield at Lake Mills was gone—eaten up by progress. The new airport, a few miles southeast, was indeed muddy, and I dared not land. I cruised over town and over the nearby lake and golf course.

After a while I flew to the site of the old airport, looped a loop or two and headed west, continuing my trip homeward. Eldon Hagen, if he was watching, would know that one of his many fledglings had stopped by to say hello.

11/Reno

I'm still not sure how I got involved in racing. Perhaps it began when I stumbled onto the aircraft requirements for the racing biplane class and found that the Starduster was qualified. Maybe it was because I had watched the Reno National Air Races several times as a spectator. Certainly I was curious about participating, but the prospect scared me a little. It was a dangerous sport.

The trip to the East Coast, stretched out by bad weather, had cut in on the time needed to prepare Second Sweetheart for racing. Less than three weeks remained before we were due on the line at Reno Stead Airfield for the Reno National Championship Air Races.

For some months my two crew members had been reading up on the rules and checking into possible changes that might legally be made to the plane and engine in order to increase the Starduster's speed.

Pat Day, explosives expert and area manager for Southwestern Explosives, was my general expediter. He saw to all the main entry forms and contacted other race pilots for information. He also lined up two sponsors: Casper White Trucks and Wyoming Central Aeroways, which had volunteered to underwrite the cost of some small engine parts and a special racing propeller.

Pat and I had become friends several years earlier through a mutual interest in homebuilt aircraft. He had had a midwing Volkswagen-powered midget racer under construction in his garage, while I had a nearly completed Starduster in mine. We traded advice and muscle frequently. His eyeball engineering talents always surprised me. He could see a mistake before it developed, or spot an existing fault and pester me until it was fixed. Wherever possible, I returned the favor.

When I invited Bob Husted to be my crew chief and take over the care of the Starduster's engine, I received a prompt "affirmative." He had helped me through some early problems with the plane and had impressed me with his knowledge and his abiding love of flying machines. Bob is one of the very few people in this world who is skinnier than I. Standing beside me, he makes me seem almost normal. On occasion we have been known to demonstrate our famous disappearing act: On cue, we turn sideways, suck in our guts and claim invisibility.

Several parcels and a stack of letters had accumulated during my three-week absence. One box contained the short, specially pitched racing prop. Sprinkled among the bills, I found an important letter from The United States Air Racing Association, assigning us racing number 17, and requiring us to report on Monday of race week to qualify plane and pilot. Additional letters from old-time race pilots Dave Forbes, Don Fairbanks and Clem Fischer held valuable advice and encouragement.

I needed the encouragement. Now that the race was near at hand, I was suffering from second thoughts. Racing around pylons was risky business. People got killed that way. The quip made by one pilot to the effect that you might get killed, but you never got hurt, offered little assurance.

Jay and I had made a special trip to the Mojave Air Races in early June to see what racing was really like. What we found surprised us both. The pilots in the racing biplane class seemed to be nice people of greatly varied, but quite ordinary background. Dave Forbes was a tall, gentle, soft-spoken airline pilot. Don Fairbanks ran a flight service in Cincinnati, and Clem Fischer did the same for many years in Nevada. Their wives were friendly and seemingly unworried about their husbands' racing. Stan Brown, Reno attorney, and C. R. "Red" Blackburn, telephone installer from Lompoc, California, both raced for the sheer joy of it. Don Beck, former test pilot, now in the construction business, raced to win—and usually did. His revolutionary, all-metal "Sorceress" usually beat out the Sundancer, flown by Logan Hines, a data processing executive from California. And finally there was Dan Mortensen, a traffic controller from Newcastle, California. "Last Place Dan," they called him. His bright yellow Smith Miniplane could barely muster 120 miles per hour. He took great delight in racing even though he generally finished last. On the final lap he always waved to the judges as he passed each of the six pylons.

There was a strange undercurrent of dissatisfaction running through the proceedings during the Mojave Race. Interclass rivalry for prize money was part of it, but anger over unfair application of rules concerning engine specifications seemed to be the main cause. I hoped the problem would heal itself before Reno rolled around.

I forced any second thoughts about racing to the back of my mind. There could be no backing out now. We had made motel reservations and Pat and Bob were both anxious to participate in the big race. I caught their fever.

For a practice area, I chose a nearby stretch of flat ground that had dirt roads at one-mile intervals, and I checked the Starduster's top speed by timing the run both ways with my stopwatch, and taking an average. If the wind quartered our path, I let the plane drift, avoiding any crab or reach. Over the two-mile course, my speed each way was simply 7,200 divided by the seconds elapsed. On the first try I got an upwind speed of 128 and a downwind of 142 for an average of 135 miles per hour. Not bad! At least I could beat Mortensen.

Although it meant endless trips to the speed course, I decided to make only one change at a time. That way I would know precisely the effect of each.

Placing tape between elevator and stabilizer did little to improve speed, and side windows to close in the cockpit did even less. Decreasing incidence by angling the front of the lower wings downward brought the speed up to 139, a four-miles-per-hour improvement. Installation of the racing propeller made little change because the expected 3,100 rpm's did not develop. We air-freighted the prop off for repitching, and in the meantime went to work on the engine.

Bob Husted installed stronger return springs on the valves, worked over the magnetos and put nonshielded, wide gap plugs on all the right mag wires. The wide gaps would ensure firing in spite of oil fouling, but would cause horrendous radio interference. To avoid that, we kept one magneto firing shielded plugs, and the radio still operated nicely with the ignition only turned to that mag.

The newly pitched prop was returned on schedule and promptly installed. It turned to 3,000 rpm's, but gave no increase in speed. The flat-pitched prop was important, however, since the original prop would turn 2,700 at racing speed, right in the middle of the bad vibration range prohibited by Lycoming, the engine's manufacturer.

The engine had been installed with down thrust and right thrust to counteract the tendency to rise and pull to the right under full throttle. For racing, it would be better to have the engine point straight away, so we hoisted it and installed washers to effect the change, and the speed went up two mph, to 141.

Upsetting news arrived from U.S.A.R.A. The race pilots were voting to boycott for higher prize money. I pleaded ignorance of the problem and entered a null vote. The extra money would be welcome, but I didn't want to see my first and only race cancelled.

The same day, I received notice that my low flying over the speed course was not appreciated. The owners of the land beneath my course objected "to that guy stormin' over ten times a day." My good buddies at the airport began calling me "Stormin' Normin," a vast improvement over "Number One Nit Wit."

Three miles from the original speed course, I found an even better two-mile stretch. Only cows occupied the land beneath.

Taping and filleting the junctions from wing to fuselage,

and gear leg to wheel pant brought another mile an hour. Disconnecting the carburetor heat hose brought an astounding increase of 4 mph. The speed now stood at a very respectable 147 mph.

We spent hours fiddling with changes in the timing, going from around 25 degrees advance to 30 degrees and then 35, and once, accidentally, to 50. Every change brought a loss of rpm's and an attendant loss of speed.

The plane was sensitive to weight. She was much slower with a full tank of gas. We calculated the minimum gas for racing to be six gallons. That would leave a two-gallon landing reserve after each heat of six laps.

We could finally think of no other changes that might bring greater speed. The plane was ready. Now it was time to see that I was ready too.

According to the rules, I must be able to take off from a dead stop at full throttle, with less than ten-foot deviation in course. I had to dive the plane to 1.3 times the maximum level speed, or about 180 mph, and pull out with 4 g's or more. I would also have to demonstrate a full roll, and show that I was safe on the pylons.

Only the last item posed a problem. I had a strong tendency to climb on low-level turns, and badly needed some practice on the race course. Lacking proper pylons, I chose three cottonwood trees spaced a quarter mile apart on some flat irrigated land and braved the wrath of the landowner by swinging about the trees full bore, trying to hold the wing a constant twenty feet off the ground while banking with the wings almost vertical. It was unnatural and difficult, requiring great concentration.

Each session with the trees left me sweating and scared, but strangely exhilarated. I wondered how I would handle flying the same steep banks at low level while flying tight formation with other planes. However, there was no way, short of racing, to practice that maneuver.

We were ready, with almost a week to spare! Then more bad news arrived from U.S.A.R.A. The old rule limiting horsepower to 125, and displacement to 290 cubic inches, had been liberalized to allow 150 horse and 320 cubes! In fact, the rule change had been effected months ago, but we were only now made aware of it.

Pat Day immediately called Dave Forbes to object. Dave,

who had just finishing readying his own Cobra biplane for the race, calmly explained that there wouldn't be more than one or two planes with the higher horsepower, and that the final legality of the change might be altered at the first pilots' meeting at Reno. Pat's anger promptly faded.

The day before we left for Reno, word arrived that the boycott had been voted down, and its originator, the president of U.S.A.R.A., was under fire from several groups, including the Reno Race promoters. The world of racing was in one hell of a mess, but the Second Sweetheart Racing Team, outfitted in brand-new bright red race jackets, was determined to persevere.

We loaded up on schedule, slept little that night, then set out early the next morning on our great excursion into the confused world of air racing.

Reno Stead Airport appeared deserted as I swung overhead. A single plane, probably Dave Forbes's Cobra, sat on the ramp and a pickup truck dusted its way past the long row of empty grandstands. There was little to indicate the excitement and controversy that would center on this lonely spot during the next few days when the Thirteenth (an omen?) Annual Reno National Air Races got underway.

The air was hot and full of bumps. I put Second Sweetheart down tail high and on the wheels with extra speed. As the plane slowed, a pickup joined my path, and I followed its lead to the ramp. A man jumped out and guided me to a parking spot beside what was indeed Dave's plane. Another gentleman walked to the cockpit and handed in a cold beer. What a welcome!

Dave wandered over, smiling. We had taken off from Elko together two hours and ten minutes earlier, but he had beaten me by twenty minutes. His new racing biplane was fast—about 30 mph faster than the Starduster.

Pat and Bob arrived as the second round of beer was passed. The hangar flying was well underway. Right in the middle of a particularly good story, Red Blackburn sputtered in with his Pitts Special. He had been pumping fuel by hand for the last hour and was worn out. Over the threshold, Red's arm and the engine died at the same time. He landed safely, rolled to a stop and we all rode out on the truck to offer aid, comfort and welcome.

Monday morning the crew of Second Sweetheart went to work. We installed the racing propeller and removed the carburetor heat hose. For some odd reason the race course was closed, so tests with the plane had to be done on the basis of rpm's and indicated air speed. On the first try, the engine wound up to a disappointing 2,900 rpm, and the air speed needle seemed stuck on 138. Bob Husted advanced the timing to 30 degrees and I tried it again, satisfied this time to see the tachometer reach 3,000 rpm, and the indicated speed 140 mph. We tucked the plane away in a corner of the hangar, gathered up a multitude of papers and headed for race headquarters to register officially.

Later we looked over the list of contestants. There were twenty planes entered in the Racing Biplane Class, and only the sixteen fastest would be permitted to race. If we ranked seventeenth, we were out of the race. Seventeen was my race number, and I hoped it had no hidden meaning, but at the moment it looked unluckier than the traditional thirteen. To qualify, we would have to beat four other planes and there were only two planes, both Smith Miniplanes, that we felt sure about.

While Pat and Bob fussed over the plane, I wandered about the ramp, worried about not qualifying, but at the same time apprehensive about closed-course pylon racing. Those damned pylons were solid, telephone poles with heavy steel culverts on top. Just touch one, and you would be dead! Dead like the T-6 pilot at last year's race. His wing tip touched the barrel and his plane ended up strewn over a hundred yards of desert sand. The prospect was unsettling.

Tuesday morning the three-mile course was declared open. Dave Forbes, Red Blackburn and I took off to run it. On the first pass I tried flying straight legs, banking steeply at each of the six corner pylons dotted along the hexagonal course, but abandoned the idea when my lap time increased, and concentrated on flying in a smooth oval. More practice would cut the time, and I decided on qualifying later in the week. There was much I had to learn about low-level pylon flying. When flying wide open at low altitude, I discovered one must push forward on the stick while banking around the pylons, quite the opposite of the back pressure I ordinarily used in turns.

That afternoon an emergency meeting was called for

Racing Biplane pilots. The controversy raging within the U.S.A.R.A. had reached a dangerous level. Several pilots, disqualified during a previous race, had arrived in Reno, ready to claim their right to race. The membership had polarized over the controversy and the four race classes had taken sides: dissident Formula One pilots, most of the Unlimited and T-6 pilots standing against the remainder. One pilot had threatened to stop the races and, fearing sabotage, we voted unanimously to hire guards to protect our planes during each night of race week.

Everything appeared normal at the mandatory general pilots' meeting the next morning. The FAA went through its rules, stressing two new favorite terms—"sterile" and "sanitary," both having to do with keeping the race course free of interlopers. The Race Director laid out the recall signals and changes in qualifying procedures. At the end of the meeting we were each asked to fill out a questionnaire concerning the mental makeup of the typical race pilot. Most pilots ignored the forms and left immediately, giving the would-be researcher one very valid bit of information: Race pilots don't give a hoot for psychological research.

The Racing Biplane pilots met again immediately after the general pilot briefing to discuss the "rules of the road." We all agreed that the overtaker was to pass well outside or well over the passee, and that all pilots should choose a track and stick with it without sudden rise or sink.

So far seven biplanes had flown their qualifying laps. We could beat two of them, Red Blackburn's Pitts, and Mortenson's Miniplane; but we had to beat two more in order to qualify for the race! We analyzed the opposition, looking for aircraft that the Starduster could top. We couldn't find one! Second Sweetheart hadn't been built for racing and carried less power than her competitors, 125 h.p. vs. 135 h.p., and in one case, 150 h.p.

Things were tense, and I was getting irritable from the pressure. Husted and I argued over engine changes, and Pat agreed with neither of us. We removed the chute, radio, emergency survival flares, tie-down ropes and logbooks. I agreed to fly without shoes, empty my pockets and swear off liquids until the plane was qualified. We moved the timing ahead to 33 degrees and taped the oil cooler three-fourths shut to raise the running temperature and thin the oil. We even covered over the rough wing walks with furnace tape!

After rolling the plane from the hangar, we drained the gas until only three gallons remained, then anxiously waited our turn, which finally arrived. We had forty minutes to test the plane and qualify. I flew the first two laps at reduced throttle, letting the oil temperature climb to 200 degrees, then opened wide and leaned the mixture to achieve maximum power. A bothersome crosswind was slowing me up and fooling me on the upwind pylons, which I was rounding dangerously close—so close I had to stand on a wing to prevent crossing over the barrel. Finally I flew a good lap, but the stopwatch read 1 minute, 19.2 seconds—much too slow. I landed and taxied to the ramp.

Bob Husted raised the cowl and eyeballed the timing back to his special 30-degree mark, and Pat Day pulled off the furnace tape that had lifted from the wing walk and was now doing more harm than good. The fellows in the gas truck quickly pumped in half a gallon and I was off again.

The engine sounded better and I had a smooth lap going— the turns were shallow and even, with the pylons passing only a few feet beyond my wing. At the home pylon I punched the watch and stole a quick look. 1:18.1—great! I cleared the watch and continued around the course, low and smooth. Past pylon six I headed straight down the home stretch, wagging my wings, signaling that I wanted to be timed for qualification on my next pass.

The starter at the home pylon waved a green flag at my approach. I punched the stopwatch at the exact moment of passage, then concentrated on each turn, approaching wide or close as the wind dictated, dropping lower for increased speed in ground effect, passing the barrels at eye level, pushing forward on the stick at every turn, concentrating, always concentrating. The lap felt good. Pylon five and six went by without a bobble, and I headed for home. The checkered flag waved as I punched the watch and zoomed sharply to altitude, letting the prop wind down before reducing throttle.

The stopwatch read an unofficial 1 minute, 17.6 seconds. It was the best the little Sweetheart and I could do, and with some luck, it would be enough to qualify. I swung in for a landing as the allotted time expired.

While Bob stowed the plane in the hangar, Pat and I walked down to check the results at race headquarters. It looked as if we were in—the last figures were being posted: No. 17, Weis, 1.17.8, speed 138.817 miles per hour! Second Sweetheart had qualified in fifteenth position! We hustled back to the hangar to hug wives and break the news to Husted, who promptly drove to town for a bottle of champagne.

We learned the starting procedures at the pilots' briefing the next morning. We would receive a ten-minute warning, then a red flag would be waved at 5, 4, 3 and 2 minutes. The assistant starter would check all planes for readiness and at one minute, the red flag would be hoisted and left up until ten seconds to go. At that point, a green flag would be hoisted. When it fell, the race was on. Any further flags would fly from the home pylon: yellow for caution, red for cancellation and black for "get off the course."

Shortly after the meeting adjourned, we were treated to a low-level jet aircraft flyby and a spectacular display by a team of female parachutists. The Reno National Air Races were underway!

The eight fastest biplane qualifiers were to fly first in the Heat 1A race, followed soon after by our race, Heat 1B. We watched closely as the planes lined up for the first heat, taking particular note of the tail-holding technique.

Don Beck in his Sorceress took an early lead, with Pat Hines close behind. Dave Forbes fought it out with Don Fairbanks for third place, and Tom Wrolstad and Tom Aberle carried on a battle behind, with Wrolstad cutting a pylon in the process. Beck, Hines and Forbes finished one, two, three, but my concern was with the technique rather than the competition. I noticed that the top pilots flew smoothly, with minimum change in bank and little variation in altitude.

Formula One races were under way as the Biplanes' Heat 1B pilots met to determine their starting positions. The fastest qualifiers were given first choice. Starting slots one through six were taken in order, and since I was the only rookie, I chose position eight, the outside slot. I figured it would put others at ease if I stayed out of the middle and be much easier for me if I only had a man on my left to look out for.

We pushed our planes the quarter mile to the starting line, feeling a 10-knot wind blow in from the south. The take-off would be tricky—right rudder would be required to prevent sliding into Red Blackburn on my left.

At the ten-minute signal, I took off my shoes and climbed aboard. Pat swung the prop a few times and the engine kicked over. Bob leaned into the cockpit for a last instrument check. The red flag signaled the five-minute warning and the assistant starter hurried down the line pointing his rolled-up flag at each pilot until he received a "thumbs up" in return. The flag waved again and he held up four fingers: The signal flashed from pilot to pilot down the line. Three minutes, and the relay was repeated. At two minutes, Pat and Bob took positions at the tail. With one minute to go, the red flag went up and stayed up. I advanced throttle to 1,500 rpm's and nervously checked the engine instruments once more—everything was normal. The red flag was down—the green flag was up—ten seconds to go! I tromped on the heel brakes, opened the throttle wide, released the parking brake and set the mixture at the predetermined mark. Eight pilots, holding full throttle, turned their heads to face the starter. Eight planes strained against brakes and tail-holding crews. Tail surfaces buffeted in hurricanelike propeller blasts. Tail crews squinted against the wash, eyeing the green flag, awaiting the moment of release.

The flag is down! Pat and Bob release the tail. At the same instant my heels come off the brakes, and Second Sweetheart leaps forward. In moments the tail rises and I concentrate on a straight takeoff run. The controls firm up and the plane lightens on the wheels. I ease back on the stick and we leave the ground. A glance to the left tells me we are in first place, but the planes in the first three positions quickly nose ahead. In slot seven, Red Blackburn is several hundred feet behind.

Win Kinner, sixty-five-year-old veteran race pilot, is still on his takeoff roll. He drifts toward the edge of the ramp, feeling the down wash of nearby planes, and his left wheel hits the dirt. The plane slews, cartwheels horizontally, and flips over. Ahead of me, five planes are strung out in a line, bending into the first pylon. I curve in behind, wide open, intent on flying a tight, smooth course. I hold wide on number two, letting the wind carry me in close. The wind is dead behind as I approach pylon three. I pull tight around the pylon and crab on the straightaway, imitating the track of the planes ahead, setting up early for pylons four and five, then easing off for six as the plane turns into the wind.

Red is just behind, heading for pylon six as I line out for the home pylon, crabbing slightly to the right. I scan Win Kinner's wrecked aircraft as I pass, noticing the empty cockpit. I thank God his plane hasn't burned and press on.

I can't seem to gain on the plane ahead. He is wide open too, trying and failing to gain on the plane in front of him. Each time I enter a straightaway I check behind and Red is always there, less than a pylon behind. Just behind him is a little black Mong, the stand-by alternate, launched right after Win Kinner cartwheeled. Below I can see the judges looking upward through the empty barrels of the pylons, checking to see if any part of the plane is visible to report it for cutting the pylon. I'm having trouble with pylon two—the wind continually puts me in too close. Twice I have to back off, then stand the plane on end to avoid cutting it. Each time I swear to take the turn wider the next lap.

Each pylon is visible between the wings as I approach, but as the bank steepens, it disappears behind the upper wing. I duck my head to prolong the view, then stretch my neck to find the pylon again as it comes into sight over the top wing, a bare 100 feet ahead. My shoulder straps inhibit the motion, but there is no time to make an adjustment. At pylon six I glance back along the course. Red is now a pylon and a half behind, with the Mong still trailing. A white flag waves as I roar by the home pylon—obviously a mistake, since I have flown only three or four laps. The next time around, the planes ahead zoom up off the course and I see the checkered flag as I pass. I can't believe the six-lap race is over.

Damn, that was fun! I finished sixth, and survived the traffic and the pylons. The fear I had expected never materialized, and a sense of pride in my accomplishment welled within me. Second Sweetheart and "Stormin' Normin" had done alright. I landed in number-six position, then taxied to the ramp for a special welcome from Jay and the crew, one of whom still carried my shoes.

The rains poured down as we pushed Second Sweetheart

into the hangar. The crowds fled and the race was canceled for the day, but the pilots, at least the biplaners, stuck around, some making adjustments, others making conversation. I asked Red what he thought of Second Sweetheart now, and he answered that it was kinda purdy, even if it was oversize. Husted, busy checking the timing, stung him by saying, "Yeah, Red. That view from the behind is really fetching, ain't it?"

Dave Forbes wandered over and presented me with the small blue card that pylon race pilots earn on completion of their first race. He welcomed me into the fraternity—a small fraternity, and an exclusive one.

Saturday was wet and drippy. A dying typhoon had limped ashore and bogged down on the California-Nevada border, but heat 1A of the Formula One race went off as scheduled. I watched with contestant's eyes, seeing only techniques, close calls and cut pylons. Judy Wagner won the race, puzzling many with her unorthodox tail-high turns that seemingly added to her speed.

Four planes took to the air for the Unlimited Medallion Race just as word was passed for the biplane pilots to get ready. We busied ourselves with the plane, and missed the Unlimited contest, which we later learned was won by John Wright at a modest 352 mph.

We rolled our planes out of the hangar as the T-6 pilots took off. You can't ignore a T-6 race because the noise is horrendous. They don't go as fast as the Formula Ones, but all that racket makes them seem faster. A bad start was called on the race, but two T-6 pilots went three laps, passing three black flags before they noticed they were racing alone.

The T-6 race was re-run as we pushed our planes down the quarter mile ramp for the Silver Race, the final race for Second Sweetheart. I had again chosen slot eight. Tom Wrolstad had been bounced down to our race for cutting a pylon in heat 1A, and Stan Brown, winner of our first race, had been moved up to the Gold, or Championship Race. Our takeoff would, of necessity, be down wind, which had increased to 10 knots. Takeoff rolls would have to be longer as a result.

We spaced out along the starting line with barely a wing span between planes, and waited for Bob Hoover to finish his aerobatic act. Given the chance, I would have traded places with him instantly. Strange how I could sit in my plane, lined up for my second big race, and still envy the guy doing aerobatics overhead.

Finally the ten-minute signal was passed down the line. Pat propped the engine, then came over to the cockpit to give me a sales talk on the advantages of flying high around the pylons. Good old Pat, always taking care of me.

Hoover skimmed past, landing on one wheel, and the assistant starter passed down the row checking alignment of the eight aircraft. At five minutes the red flag went up and the thumbs-up ritual began. Red Blackburn looked our way as I passed my shoes to Husted. His eyes widened, his mouth dropped and his mustache wobbled a silent disapproval. I gave him a thumbs-up. He grinned and returned the sign, resembling a character out of World War I—leather helmet, scarf, eyes full of devil-may-care.

I tightened the seat belt and adjusted the shoulder harness. At the one-minute signal I went to half throttle. Pat and Bob gave me parting taps on the helmet and took position at the tail. The red flag dropped and the green went up. The plane strained at full throttle, eager to get away. When the green flag dropped, Second Sweetheart surged, accelerating rapidly. We were off in seconds, leading the field briefly. Half way to the first pylon, six of us were flying abreast; then four planes drew ahead and formed in line. The black Mong to my left gained the edge, and I swung wide to avoid his wash.

The pilot of the Mong was flying smoothly this time, avoiding his earlier square corners. His lead increased slightly. At pylon three I checked behind. Red was just rounding number one. I concentrated on my flying, hoping to catch the Mong with six smooth laps. If I could close on him, he would probably revert to his old style, and I would have him.

The wind moved me in to pylon six, and I backed off, then tightened up, banking steeply and losing speed in the process. The wind tended to carry me wide but I anticipated by aiming to the inside, feeling the drift as Second Sweetheart rounded the pylon a dozen feet out, barrel level with the lower wing tip. Pat's advice on flying high was forgotten. Though I had no chance of winning, the heat of the race would not permit conservative flying. I had the wind figured out, staying wide on five and six, and boring in on two and three. The Mong was closer now, less than a pylon ahead. I checked oil pressure and temperature on the next straightaway, adjusted the mixture, noting the tachometer bouncing at 3,150 rpm, then leaned forward to concentrate on a smooth turn around pylons one, two and three. Wrolstad, flying 20 mph faster than the Sweetheart, passed me high and wide, but I never saw him. My eyes were where they belonged—on the pylons.

The Mong was even closer as we rounded number six and headed past home. Damn! There was the white flag—only one lap left, not enough to catch him. Second Sweetheart and I would finish in sixth place again. I bored around the last lap 15 feet off the ground anyway, in a vain attempt to catch the Mong, careful to rise to legal, eye-level height as I rounded the barrels, but I could only watch helplessly as he took the checkered flag and zoomed to altitude. I waggled my wings to acknowledge the checkered flag as I passed the home pylon, then climbed steeply and curved in for a landing.

Pilots and crews, all in high spirits, gathered in the biplane hangar. We raced the race again, passing our compliments and criticisms, and taking the same in exchange. Don Perri, pilot of the black Mong, offered congratulations. I said kind words about his flying, then claimed I would have had him if there had been two more laps. Red disagreed: "Hell, the way you guys were flying, two more laps and I'd of passed both of ya!"

I felt a great sense of satisfaction. The race had been a test, and I had passed. Other pilots apparently felt the same. It showed in their actions and in their words. Egos were at rest because there was nothing left to prove.

Perhaps racers race because of the wonderful feeling that follows a successful confrontation with one's inner fears, a feeling of measuring up in a company of brave companions. Certainly it isn't the money. Our share of the purse was a bit over $500, and our expenses were triple that figure—even the championship purse for Racing Biplanes was less than $2,000. It couldn't be the recognition either, for there was little recognition offered, or accepted. A few reporters waited outside the hangar, but fewer pilots chose to leave the company of fellow pilots for an interview. No, it's not the money or the glory, it's something else—a feeling of unshakable confidence in oneself that brings the racer back to race again.

12/Pushing the Limits

All things have a limit. I thought I had pressed the Starduster's capabilities to the limit, but in reality I had taxed only my own. My limit was that fine line between propriety and fear. The Starduster's limit, if reached, would be structural failure. The Starduster had suffered not the slightest bend or give. It was time to push the limit—my limit. If I were to realize my dream of flying professional aerobatics, it was time to perfect some top-notch maneuvers for my act.

Part of my enthusiasm was due to Neil Williams' new book on aerobatics. His explanations concerning simple maneuvers coincided with my own. We were both self-taught, but he had progressed far beyond my rudimentary level of competency. He could explain a complex move in a way that made you want to jump into the plane and try it immediately. Since Second Sweetheart was not capable of sustaining inverted flight, some of the enticing maneuvers were beyond reach. However, the list of possibilities was still considerable.

Perhaps the most exciting was the "dreaded" inverted spin, which, according to the new book, was not to be dreaded at all. The design of most planes made the spin and the recovery easier inverted than upright. Having frightened myself with accidental inverted spins, I was determined to conquer that feeling by doing a few on purpose.

The air was calm and cool 7,000 feet above Golden Eye Reservoir. Smooth pasture land fronted the lake, offering safe landing in case the engine stopped completely. I circled, checked my procedure, and tugged the chute straps tight; then pulled up sharply, as if entering a loop, and eased the stick forward, pulling the throttle all the way back. Speed dribbled away quickly as I held the nose high, still inverted. She shuddered on the edge of a stall and I jammed in full right rudder and full forward stick. The world whirled and I counted the turns. After the second revolution, I jammed full opposite rudder, and when the rotation stopped, pulled the stick back to point the nose down.

The old master, Neil Williams, was right. Spinning head down was easier than upright. There was no feel of being thrown out, and the plane showed no reluctance to recover. The big difference was visual. When upright, earth and sky seem to circle the plane, but inverted, no sky showed at all!

I tried another inverted spin of two turns, then three, and finally four, climbing each time to 7,000 feet and finishing up at just under 5,000 feet. The fishermen a mile below no doubt figured the spins were simply more of the same old upright variety they had seen me do at lower level, and probably wondered at my sudden conservative attitude.

The 125 horses in the Starduster's nose didn't provide much of an up line. If I dived to 160, then smoothly pointed straight up, she would climb perhaps 1,000 feet before dying and falling back for lack of thrust. Falling back, tail first, in what is appropriately termed a tail slide, could have serious consequences. The maneuver is safe as long as power is continued. The air blast from the propeller permits the elevators to act quite normally for that short interval before the craft swaps ends and heads straight for the ground, nose first.

But with power off, it's quite a different story. As the plane slides backward, the reverse flow of air exerts strong forces on the elevators, tending to force them full travel up or down. If the pilot is caught napping, the force is great enough to snatch the control stick out of his hand and let the control surfaces bang hard against the stops. The damage can render the plane uncontrollable; hence the bad stories and warnings concerning tail slides, especially accidental tail slides.

There are two ways to recover from a tail slide, and I was determined to try them both. From maximum altitude, I dove to 160 and pulled up, checking both wings for horizon position, to ensure a vertical track. As speed dwindled, I drew the throttle back, grabbed the stick in both hands and firmed my feet on the rudder pedals. The air noise diminished. For a moment it was quiet. Then the string on the "I" strut streamed out in front and air flew into the cockpit from the rear. We slid back, gaining more speed than I wanted. I was pointed too precisely perpendicular and the plane could not decide which way to flip. I pulled back slightly on the stick to help the plane commit itself to an upright recovery. Immediately the stick came all the way back. I could not hold it, only ease the bump against the stop. Instantly the tail whipped up and the nose down—over correcting itself until we were nearly inverted—then swung back, nose headed for the ground.

I brought the plane level and felt out the controls, even loosened the shoulder straps and swiveled about to study the elevators. Everything appeared normal.

I tried several more, taking care to climb at 85 degrees rather than 90. The slide back was shorter, and the stick forces easier to combat.

The second variety of tail slides involved recovery "on the back," with head down and eyeballs out. I pointed the plane straight up again, but leaned back at about 100 degrees this time, chopped the power and held the stick firmly, a bit forward of center. The plane slid back, then abruptly whipped upside down, oscillated and pointed down. Like the inverted spin, the advertisements were exaggerated. The move, although sloppy and imprecise, was fun and easy.

Later, a thorough ground inspection of the tail assembly and elevator control linkage showed no signs of over stress. I counted it lucky that the first tail slide was more violent than

148

The birth of the Starduster: Laying out the fuselage halves

The Starduster completed: Ready for its first flight

Learning: "We flew the canyons and waved at countless fishermen."

Practicing for Reno: A tree makes a forgiving pylon

Some of my competitors: The Rocky Mountain Championship,
Longmont, Colorado

Wade, Jay and the deputy sheriff help load the wrecked Starduster
onto a flatbed

The new Starduster: Doing a knife-edge
—just like old Speed Holman

needed. Now I could trust the plane's structural integrity for properly executed slides.

Between practice sessions, I studied the possibility of installing a smoke system. A separate tank could be installed in the upper wing, with a flop tube and double vents. A rechargeable battery could be installed anywhere, and it would drive an electric fuel pump to send a special oil—corvus oil—through tubes to each exhaust stack. It involved a lot of work, and quite a little extra weight. I decided to postpone the project until winter.

Friends who fly straight and level, in aircraft designed to fly straight and level, are apt to question my abiding passion for aerobatics. Why, they want to know, am I determined to try such things as inverted spins and tail slides—things they were always taught to avoid at all costs. My explanations are generally unsatisfactory: I try because I feel I must.

The plane is like any new toy—a bicycle, for example. Remember when you owned one and you learned to ride it, at the expense of a few scraped knees and elbows? One day you had to try riding "no hands," even if your parents thought it foolhardy. Perhaps you even tried a wheelie.

I guess the feeling starts at birth. Every new skill reveals a new challenge. Once you can crawl, you strive to walk, and walking, you must learn to run, then jump and dance. It is when you stop the process—when you think you have experienced it all—that you begin to grow old. A challenge is necessary to the way I wish to live, and my challenge just happens to be aerobatics.

But isn't it risky? Perhaps. As Thoreau said, "It is life near the bone where it is sweetest."

Torque rolls are beautiful and feel just the way they look, but the control motions are strange. Once pointed vertically, full aileron is cranked in and the plane begins to roll. With eyes fixed on the left wings, the plane seems stationary, and the horizon becomes a passing blur. Prompt fore and aft motions of the stick keep the wings perpendicular to the whirling horizon. So far everything is easy, but soon the left wing begins to ride too high. Left rudder will bring it down, and when you've overdone it, a touch of right rudder will bring it back on the horizon.

Handling the stick and rudder during a torque roll is like patting your head and rubbing your stomach. Once learned, a new refinement can be added. When the plane reaches the top and starts to slide back, the ailerons should be reversed so the wings can unscrew their way down, preserving the rotation. Other control motions remain the same, since full power still puts normal air blast over the tail. But only for a while. Soon the backward motion brings on more reverse flow of air than the prop wash can handle, and the plane sags over and oscillates to a downward path.

Some planes can achieve three or four rolls on the upline, hang on the prop for another, then rotate two or three more turns on the way down. The Starduster, with a lesser roll rate due to its lack of four ailerons, does well to get a three-quarter roll up and a half roll down. It's not much of a torque roll, so I prefer to call it a "rolling tail slide."

Whifferdill! What an exotic name for a maneuver. I wanted to learn the maneuver if only to make use of the term. When I finally found out what it was from an English friend, I realized I had been doing it for more than a year. It was nothing but a barrel roll that has its mind changed midway, or you could call it a super-steep lazy eight, so steep the wings go past vertical to precisely inverted, then return. It is a long sweeping reversing maneuver that keeps you pleasantly in your seat.

Square loops, diamond loops and eight-sided loops are simple from the pilot's seat, but viewed from outside, first efforts look more like rectangles, squashed boxes and ellipses.

The problem is with the timing. Speed changes are drastic, and to draw equal sides, one must fly for unequal times. For example, the first leg of a diamond loop: Upward at 45 degrees should be held for a count of three, then the plane rotated 90 degrees with elevator, and the new course held for a count of five; another 90 degrees and held for a count of four (the engine and gravity are now working together), then a final 90 degrees held for a count of two, then level. A ground observer can suggest slight changes in count and angle, and when mastered, the maneuver will look grand from the ground but seem all wrong from the cockpit.

During the exit from a maneuver, the controls sometimes take on a new stiffness and the wires a new higher-pitched howl. A glance at the airspeed indicator explains it all—a new top speed has been reached. I make it a practice to check both ailerons for incipient flutter (they would look extra fat) before reducing throttle and pulling out. Later I move the red "Do not exceed speed" line up to a new position on the dial.

Climbing in and out of the Starduster was still a graceless act. In spite of special precautions, I frequently ran the stick up my pant leg. Even when I toed the stick to the side and out of the way, the wind on the ailerons would move it back in time to match the planting of my foot. I tried doing it on purpose and found it difficult. It was much easier by accident. Some day I planned to rework the trim system so the stick wouldn't ride at center travel, but in the meantime, the best I could do was leave all my flared britches in the closet and wear the tight-cuffed pants that had gone out of style four years ago.

The new maneuvers demanded much time to bring me to competence, then far more time to achieve a measure of precision. The inverted spin was the easiest. I sprinkled that maneuver in among the difficult moves to maintain confidence.

When I told Pat Day about the joys of spinning upside down, he had to have a demonstration. Jay, also curious, rode out to the practice area with Pat.

I could see them standing beside the vehicle as I climbed to 5,000 feet. Any higher, I reasoned, and the plane would present too small an image.

On the top of the loop, I pulled the throttle back, but not all the way—the engine would die from fuel starvation anyway. She entered the spin nicely, and after two turns I kicked opposite rudder. Nothing happened! I kicked again and nothing happened! Something was awfully wrong! I could see blue sky and hear a strange fluttering-roaring sound. I considered slipping the belts and bailing out, a thought that had never crossed my mind before. Could I clear the plane? Perhaps the spinning plane would wrap the canopy up into a useless ball. Maybe I was already too low to jump.

Suddenly I understood what was happening. The funny sound was the engine running, and that made the spin flatten up and bring the sky in view.

Quickly I yanked the throttle back, jammed the rudder again, and . . . but I honestly can't recall everything I tried. Anyway, the nose dropped and the spin slowed. I pulled the stick back much too soon, but the plane responded in its own time. I leveled quickly and checked my altitude. The altimeter read 1,000 feet, which was 2,500 feet lower than I had intended!

I milled about, letting the adrenaline run down, wondering how an engine without an inverted system could run upside down. Of course! Rotation would throw the fuel away from the axis, and that would be forward to the engine! I should have taken off all the throttle at the top of the loop.

By the time I reached the airport, I realized the experience had given me some valuable insights into the nature of inverted flat spins. The spin would flatten with power and return to normal without power. Admittedly, some planes will not return to a normal spin even when power is shut down, but the Sweetheart, thank heaven, was one of the safe ones. The inverted flat spin would be a good maneuver to practice sometime later—but now there were other, more interesting maneuvers to master.

It was time to try out the Starduster's flight characteristics in odd attitudes with radical control positions. Perhaps we could invent a new maneuver like the tail stand the Waco driver demonstrated at Oshkosh.

I tried entering a continuous snap roll from different angles and attitudes. Most of the results were disappointing, but when I entered that maneuver from a nearly vertical position, strange things happened. For example, a spin would start normally, but as the speed died, the spin died, and we fell out in some unpredictable attitude. (At times it felt as though we were briefly in an inverted spin, and since I kept the power on, and there was a chance the spin could go flat, I kept plenty of altitude.) I experimented with different entry speeds, angles off the vertical, and tried the spin in both directions. I failed to duplicate the Waco's moves, but in the process, I came upon a new, apparently original maneuver. Perhaps it's something only the Starduster can accomplish. I named it the "Boilermaker."

Heading up at 80 degrees, I waited for the speed to drop to 110 mph, then quickly put the plane into a spin to the right. She spun a turn or two, died on top, and for a short while lay flat on her back with no rotation. Then as the plane started to fall back, I fed in whatever control it took to prolong the float while torque from the engine brought on a slow spin to the left. If done properly, the controls ended up with stick forward and full rudder deflection, precisely the requirements for an inverted flat spin, which was exactly what the plane was doing. And it was entered from a normal spin going straight up! I never gave the flat spin time to fully develop. A half turn or so, and I chopped power and pointed her down.

Spinning to the right is at odds with the natural tendency to spin left due to propeller torque. At the apex, torque takes over, stops rotation and causes a slow inverted flat spin to set in to the left. Done properly, the plane stops dead at the top, flat on its back, then slowly unscrews its way down, still flat on its back.

Some of the fellows from the Experimental Aircraft Association—the EAA—were flying a replica of Lindbergh's *Spirit of Saint Louis* about the country, much the way Lindy had toured around after his Atlantic flight fifty years earlier. The plane was due in Casper at noon, and quite a crowd had gathered at the airport to see the show. Several homebuilt aircraft were on display, mine included. This time I played it smart and surrounded the plane with one-inch-wide fluorescent surveyor's tape, to keep people from looking with their hands instead of with their eyes. Somehow the unused portion of the tape was left in the cockpit. it fell into the fuselage and much later, at a very crucial time, I would find it in a critical place.

When word arrived that the *Spirit of Saint Louis* would be two hours late, I volunteered to entertain the crowd with a little aerobatic demonstration during the wait. The FAA was on hand, and I had a low-level waiver, so the legalities were quickly satisfied.

At the first break in the traffic, the tower gave me the go-ahead. It was a real kick to go through the maneuvers I had thoroughly perfected—the ones proven safe at low altitude. Bottoming out at 1,000 feet, I passed from loop to hammerhead to whifferdill to barrel roll, frequently reversing with the Sweetheart's easy half-snap split "S," then going on to the cubans, point rolls, slow rolls and snaps, with one snap roll while going straight down. As a finale, I dove for speed, and then pointed her up and spun her into one of my better boilermakers. It felt so good I did another. Now if the crowd had been larger, and I were receiving a healthy fee . . . maybe sometime.

A month later, after much practice on diamond loops and rolling tail slides, I moved on to a couple of simple maneuvers called the pullover and pushover. Both are entered going straight up, and both end up going straight down. The pull and push refer to the stick motions. The pullover is a tall skinny loop; the pushover is the same shape but the plane—as in an outside loop—is upright at the apex. At that moment, the plane and pilot are subjected to negative g's. The pilot is thrust up against the belts, his neck stretches, and his eyeballs bulge. Anything loose tends to rise.

It was at such a moment that I found my long lost roll of surveyor's tape lying unknown in the tail of the aircraft. It rose into the gap between elevator actuating arm and fin post. (The gap was there because the elevator was in the down position.) The pushover and the down line all seemed normal, but when I applied back stick to pull out, my movement met sudden solid resistance. Luckily, enough up elevator was available so that by using reduced throttle I was able to pull out very gradually and get back to a level attitude at a safe distance from the ground. But the problem now was to get back to the airport, get it on the ground, then find out what the hell was causing the blockage.

I held hard back stick, compressing whatever the mysterious object was. I briefly considered jockeying about, but discarded the idea. If the object shifted, the chances were 50-50 that the problem would worsen. I would have to land holding the stick against the blockage and using only my throttle to control my descent. It would have to be a wheel landing, but at least that was my normal landing style anyway.

I told the tower about my problem, and asked for a "no delay" straight in approach. They obliged by delaying several other planes, then sent the crash trucks screaming onto the runway. Their presence was comforting, but, as it turned out, unnecessary. Even with a jammed elevator, the Starduster landed as sweetly as I could have wished.

When I removed the inspection plates and found the offending tape roll, I could see that even its tough inner core had been deeply dented—evidence of the furious back pressure I had been applying to the stick. For the second time I resolved to inspect the belly for debris before each aerobatic flight.

I carried that bulky, deformed roll in my pocket for two weeks like a guilty sailor, neck slung with a dead albatross, hoping its discomfort would serve as a permanent reminder.

13/Wheel of Fortune

It was 7 A.M. on the first of January, and the thermometer stood at ten below zero. The two hairdryers humming away in the blanket-covered engine compartment seemed to have little effect against the bitter cold. I busied myself stowing tent, sleeping bag, air mattress, tie-downs and survival gear, then pastered over the oil-cooler with furnace tape.

By nine o'clock the engine oil temperature had finally climbed into the green. I removed the hairdryers and blankets, pulled on an extra jacket, snugged the windproof hood and slid my flying helmet over the top, slung a scarf about my neck, pulled on heavy gloves and climbed into the cold cockpit. The engine started on the line-hand's first pull and I sat waiting for it to warm completely, wondering if I could stand the cold temperatures at altitude. I hadn't planned to leave on the coldest day of the year.

The decision to go had been an easy one. The race promoters had offered me $300 to put on two aerobatic acts, and a few more dollars' prize money if I entered the races to fill out the field. Racing no longer thrilled me, but I found it impossible to turn down my first chance to fly aerobatics for decent money. Besides, the races were to be held in Mexicali, Mexico, where the weather should be warm. It was to be the first Mexicali International Air Race, and I would be the feature performer. They expected a crowd of 10,000.

The official who had checked my qualifying dive, as well as my rolls and the extra goodies I had thrown in at Reno, was the man who had made the offer. The little string attached—the requirement that I also race—would violate my promise to Jay of no more racing. Luckily, she understood my deep desire to fly the air show and I was granted a "stay of promise" for just this race. Strangely enough, Jay had no worries concerning my aerobatics, but she reasoned that when racing, my life was in the other fellows' hands—and she didn't trust the other fellows.

I felt a bit guilty about Mexicali, however, for it was there that I gave my middle-fingered salute the year before. Back then I dared not enter the country for fear the plane might be confiscated, but now the Governor of Mexico had sent each of the race pilots a personal invitation.

We cleared the ground at 9:30 A.M., and headed cold and straight for Rock Springs. A little fuel, some hot coffee and we were up again, flying through the paralyzing cold. The heater couldn't keep up with the frigid air rushing by, and shivers set in as we left Wyoming and entered the State of Utah. I upped the cruise settings to raise the temperature and shorten the flight time.

Clouds took over the sky and the temperature dropped even lower. My hand shook, sending small pulses through the controls. Finally, we slid down the notch between Heber City and Provo. The lower altitude was a relief as the temperature rose to near the freezing level.

The airport at Nephi, Utah, was untended, but a phone call brought a sheriff's deputy immediately. I gassed up the Sweetheart and headed out, pleased with the deputy's friendliness, wondering what the town was like. I would find out all about it eight days later.

Mountain shadows were growing long as we landed at

Cedar City, Utah, a pleasant place to spend the night. The hardest part of the trip was behind me. Only two legs and a hop remained before the bright Mexican sun would warm my bones.

The next morning was again cold and the engine slow to fire. It was ten o'clock before we cleared Cedar City and headed south. Twenty miles out, we passed over land badly cut by canyons. In one of those canyons, nearly fifty years ago, mail pilot Maury Graham was forced to land in midwinter. He and his wrecked plane were found the following spring. Maury had managed to walk six miles before exhaustion brought him down, to die alone in a barren land.

The rough country ended abruptly and we descended to the flat warmth of the Nevada desert. Boulder City was only half an hour ahead. We had been this route before. This time the Air Force and Nellis Field received a wide berth as we detoured through the Valley of Fire, then slid along the west shore of Lake Mead.

At Boulder City I removed the tape from the cooler, and stowed my windbreaker and gloves. Then I pointed the nose straight south and watched the Colorado River meander along a dozen miles to the east. The land below me turned from tan to brown, and erupted into tusks of igneous rock.

It was hot when we landed at Blythe, California. After gassing up, I dawdled over coffee in the flight shack, giving the engine time to cool. Because of the low elevation and high temperature it had become balky and hard to start.

I checked the parking brake and found it still full on, then looked about to see if anyone was available to swing the prop. Not a soul. I thought briefly of tying down the tail, but no ground loops were visible nearby.

With throttle well cracked and ignition on, I stood between wing and prop and pulled her through. She coughed, coughed again, then quit firing altogether, obviously loaded up with a heat-induced rich mixture. With ignition off and throttle wide open, I pulled the prop through a dozen times, then retarded the throttle, turned on the ignition, and tried again. Again the engine coughed and died.

Sweat began to gather under my long johns. The engine failed again and I looked about for help. There was still no one in sight. I decided there was no point in trying to start her until I had leaned out the mixture, so I set full throttle and started to pull the prop. I was on the third pull of twelve when, to my horror, the engine fired! My God, I'd left the ignition on! I frantically ran for the wing tip. The tail was already coming up as I headed for the cockpit. With the engine at full bore, the prop was beginning to chew its way into the blacktop. My first leap at the cockpit failed. Now the plane was crawling toward a gas truck! On the second or third jump, I managed to get on the wing and claw my way over the cockpit coaming to yank the throttle back and cut the ignition.

Now there were lots of people around, bombarding me with accusing eyes and condemning silence. I was sick. In a thousand hours of flying I had never hurt an airplane. Now I had demolished a prop and come perilously close to blowing up a gas truck.

I had to wait in Blythe two days before a new prop arrived from Phoenix. It came by air-freight at 2 P.M. on the last day to check in at Mexicali. Takeoff was extra quck, and the climb out spectacular. The new prop was better than the old one. The cruise speed was a few miles slower, but that mattered little. I wasn't interested in racing or cross country these days, just aerobatics, and the new prop would make a big improvement in my vertical performance.

The General Taboada International Airport lay just a few miles south of the border amid land checkerboarded by irrigation. I landed and Bob Downey, Formula One pilot and coordinator of the races, directed me to parking. Good old Red Blackburn, walrus mustache droopy as ever, sauntered over to stammer out a welcome. I began to feel at home.

Red hustled me directly to customs to cancel my flight plan and enter the country officially. The customs man spoke no English and I could speak no Spanish, so we communicated by writing numbers, adding question marks if not sure. When finished, the immaculately uniformed agent stood at attention, shook my hand, and offered an official welcome, repeating "*piloto, piloto, race piloto.*" He pronounced it "pee-low-toe."

The course was parallel to the single runway, and quite close in. The race promoter, uninhibited by the Mexican equivalent of the FAA, requested that all races and aerial acts be held as close to the crowd as possible. He even suggested that the scheduled clown act and my aerobatic act be held next to, or right over the crowd. The races took on a barnstorming atmosphere, and the *pilotos* loved it.

Mexicali, a brown and dusty city of half a million people, sprawled across the flats a dozen miles west of the airport. The houses on the outskirts of town seemed temporary; rusty corrugated sheets and loose-fitted boards that spoke well for the climate. Except for the highways, streets were powdered dust or clinging mud, depending upon the weather. At the center of town, the buildings became substantial. Statues stood in midstreet, and multistoried motels rose on both sides of the dusty boulevards. One of the motels became the race pilots' home for the weekend.

Early Friday morning a small crowd gathered at the airport to watch the qualifying rounds. A trial run on the course showed that Pylon Six had to be moved inward to prevent overflight of the runway. That was very important, since ordinary traffic would continue during the races—ordinary traffic being four jetliners, plus the sporadic arrival and departure of a few dozen smaller craft each day.

It felt good to round the pylons again. Although I hadn't made changes for speed, I knew I was going in excess of 135 mph. However, the timers claimed 176 kilometers per hour, or 109 mph. It was ridiculous, but they insisted their figures were right. Their electronic timers could not be wrong. Obviously the course was longer than measured. I agreed to let things stand, hoping the timers would at least be consistent.

During a break in the action, I went up to practice my aerobatic act, low and close in as requested. The new prop and the dense air turned the Sweetheart into a tiger. Tommy Thomason, a friend of Red's from Lompoc, California, tried out his drunk act, and I watched people duck and run as he worked his Aeronca Champ in close. A jetliner landed, then took off, while trial runs continued without break. Formula one racers and jetliners passed in opposite directions a few hundred feet apart, but only the Americans considered it unusual.

At midday, the arrival of the California contingent—having been delayed by weather—brought the roster of racers to full complement. They hastened to qualify their planes. It was well after sunset before the planes were tucked away in the hangar. We stood in the gathering darkness and talked until the air turned cold.

Dave Forbes had brought his Cobra biplane. His wife had flown down in a Cessna, and both planes were scheduled to race. Dan Mortenson, whose little yellow Smith Miniplane had failed to qualify at Reno, was there, but he wouldn't be eliminated this time. He had a new screamer—a Mong that he believed capable of more than 160 mph.

All the old gang from Reno was here and the evening was a jolly reunion. We took over the small bar and café at the motel, much to the discomfort of the regular customers and the waiters, who were not happy with the noise and the shenanigans. We were "ugly Americans" for the evening.

The next morning we were heroes. That's what the announcer on the public address system said. He spoke in Spanish, but the words *"brave, grande, valiente, hero,"* and *"famoso piloto"* came through unmistakably. The audience must have believed every word, for we were met with wide-eyed approval as we pushed our planes along the edge of the crowd. We formed a line in front of the crowd and stood for introductions, waving whenever the announcer pointed in our direction.

Dan Mortensen and I were in the fourth race, along with four other bipes of similar speed. They let me off first with a handicap of ten seconds—but in less than a lap Mortensen, in his green and yellow hornet, zipped by wagging his wings in revenge for Reno. Then everyone else passed me—but what the hell, I was here to put on an aerobatic act, not to race. I flew across the finish line on knife-edge to cover my embarrassment.

During the Formula One race, one of the pilots passed through a bad wake and severely damaged a disc in his spine. He managed a landing at the far end of the runway, but it was some time before anyone realized he needed help. Finally he was transferred to an ambulance and taken to Mexicali.

That made a few of us curious as to the quality of the crash truck and fire-fighting facilities. We wandered over for a look and found a frightening lack of preparation. There were no asbestos suits laid out, and no one sat ready in the cabs. In fact, the crews were scattered about, enjoying the festivities. Worst of all, the fire

161

truck had no foam, only water, quite useless on gasoline fires. The freedom from regulations that we were all enjoying apparently had some drawbacks.

Clem Fischer had to pull out of his race after a few turns about the pylons. A strange noise developed in the engine and the power fell off, making an immediate landing necessary. We viewed his engine, tracking the dripping oil to a split crankcase, a problem much too complicated to permit immediate repair. He began making plans to drive down the following week to load his sick airplane on a flatbed for the long haul home.

The stock plane race was on the final lap as I took off for my aerobatic act. I circled, scanning the long line of spectators as the stock racers strung out for a landing. Citizens of Mexicali and nearby towns lined the south side of the runway. Most of them had never seen an air show, but then I had never performed before such a large crowd. We made a good match. I hoped they would applaud my mistakes as well as my better executions.

The last of the stock racing planes landed. That was the signal for the announcer to introduce the Starduster and its pilot.

The moment is ours!

From 1,000 feet we slice down, building speed, heading for a point just off the edge of the crowd. The speed reaches 160 and the wires sing. We level, then quickly drop the right wing until it points precisely to the ground, giving the crowd a full view of the Sweetheart's red and white scalloped wing. Two hundred feet above the runway we race by the long line of spectators, flying on knife-edge—flying sideways, just like old Speed Holman.

A mild buffet sets in, and it's time to level and climb steeply to 800 feet, half snap upside down, dive to low level and make a slow roll on the return pass in front of the crowd.

On the climb out there's time to check the card for the next two moves, a full cuban followed by a loop. My notes on the card tell me I need 900 feet and 100 mph. We have it. Now kick rudder and ride the wing over through a reverse, then slide back down, looking for 160, and then up and over, float the top, wait for the 45-degree line inverted, then roll upright, hold the line, level, check the altitude—300 feet—safe enough, then pull up and repeat.

It's all so easy when you know how. It's the knowing how

that's difficult. We are through the loop with ease, and I scan the runway below, checking for alignment. A Cessna single-engine has just landed and is rolling out a few hundred feet beneath the bottom of my loop. I feel the wind in my face as we float freely across the top of a hammerhead. And they are paying me money to do this!

The biplane grin is back, and I hold on to it, high on the fulfillment of my boyhood dream—a dream I had always clung to but never really thought was attainable. This, for me, was what it was all about, my "high flight," and I recall the marvelous words of John Gillespie Magee, Jr.*:

HIGH FLIGHT

> Oh, I have slipped the surly bonds of earth
> And danced the skies on laughter-silvered wings;
> Sunward I've climbed, and joined the tumbling mirth
> Of sun-split clouds—and done a hundred things
> You have not dreamed of—wheeled and soared and swung
> High in the sunlit silence. Hov'ring there,
> I've chased the shouting wind along, and flung
> My eager craft through footless halls of air.
> Up, up the long, delirious, burning blue
> I've topped the windswept heights with easy grace
> Where never lark, or even eagle flew.
> And, while with sildent, lifting mind I've trod
> The high untrespassed sanctity of space,
> Put out my hand, and touched the face of God.

The hammerhead comes out crooked and I snap back to reality. I repeat the move, doing it right, then climb for my finale. From 1,500 feet we roar down until the airspeed reads 175, then pull up and point for the sky. As the speed drops to 110, I kick rudder and hold a bit of back pressure on the stick. We enter a spin going straight up. The spin slows, stops and we fall back down, inverted, beginning a slow spin in the opposite direction. The Boilermaker! We float down inverted a bit longer than usual,

---

*From *Masterpieces of Religious Verse*. Reprinted by permission of Harper & Row, Publishers.

giving the folks their money's worth, then point for the ground, feeling great.

Everything had gone well, a glorious experience. I felt like flying a few more maneuvers in celebration, but my time slot was used up. I landed, and taxied to the stand for my after-act introduction. The audience's applause was generous and, to me, intoxicating.

The crowd gathered again early on Sunday, the final day of the races. I walked through the throng taking note of the great difference between Mexicali and Reno race enthusiasts. The Mexicans were more inclined to smile and less apt to push and shove. Of course the children were special. Bright, sparkly-eyed and shy, they tended to hide from my camera. Smiling parents coaxed them forward with much confusion in communication, but always with great good humor.

Photographers were everywhere. Yesterday we had politely posed for them, assuming they were from the local press. Today they were selling us the photos, and their business was booming.

At Bob Downey's suggestion, I agreed to put on an extra aerobatic act just after the biplane race. In fact, we cooked up what should have been a very fitting act. It was the *touristas*, the Mexican name for a delicate problem we all had developed from drinking the local water, that gave me the idea.

I planned to fly in front of the crowd, tossing out three-foot lengths of toilet paper while the announcer explained that I had the *touristas*. Then, at 1,000 feet, I would throw out a whole roll and cut it up with the prop, while running through some aerobatics. As the first roll drifted to the ground, I would make one last pass, climb up and toss out another roll, with the announcer making additional quips. We figured the fifteen-minute comedy-aerobatic routine was just what the show needed. Bob went over the plans with the announcer while I located the rolls of paper.

The final race for the "slow" biplanes was about to start. I sat in the cockpit, engine running, adjusting the two rolls of toilet paper tucked into the front of my jacket. My shirt pockets were stuffed with the three-foot lengths. I felt like a pigeon with a chest problem.

I was second in line, waiting to take off fifteen seconds

after the man ahead. The first plane left and I counted the seconds; one thousand one, one thousand two. At twelve, I opened the throttle wide, watching Art Williams hold up the green flag. When my count reached fifteen, I eased the brakes and began to roll. I must have anticipated, for Art cautioned me with a push of the flag. Without thinking, I instinctively did the one thing I should not have done—I jammed on the brakes!

Up came the tail. For a moment I thought I had it saved, but then the tail bobbed up again and the prop struck. Once the prop began grinding into the blacktop, no amount of back stick would bring the tail down. Belatedly, I pulled the throttle back, turned off the ignition and sat there hoping it was all just a bad dream. They rolled me off the runway while I held my helmeted head in my hands.

El stupido piloto—that was me! No one could say anything that compared to the hell I gave myself. I searched for an excuse, an alibi to explain the mistake away, then accepted the fact that I had simply goofed.

It hurt—really hurt—pushing the plane back past the endless and pointing crowd. I had wanted to be remembered as the fellow who did the aerobatics. Now I was the guy who bent his prop.

The announcer was busy calling the race. As it ended, he began the warmup on my toilet paper act. I walked over and tried to explain. He didn't understand, so I pulled out the two rolls of toilet paper, gave them to him and pointed to my damaged propeller. He pointed at the propeller, then at me. I nodded my head, feeling terrible. I didn't much like myself.

It turned out that Clem Fischer had no need for a propeller on his crippled plane, and was willing to let me borrow it for my final show and for the trip home to Casper. His offer seemed a godsend, but it proved to be my third, and final, mistake.

My final aerobatic act began satisfactorily, but the keen edge was removed by lingering embarrassment. I forced myself to concentrate on the point rolls and the hammerheads, and I managed to fly the hesitation hammerhead with some flair. On the downline I snap rolled the plane in one of Rancher Steinle's "shot down maneuvers" and was startled to see a glider in tow pass below. The shock caused the snap to come out crooked. But separation was adequate, so I climbed for altitude, reading my Aresti card. We roared down, leveled and flew an arching four-point Hoover roll, then angled, rolled again, and half snapped a turn about.

Now I was with it. I flew some of the "hundred moves you've never dreamed of" that John Gillespie Magee wrote about. We wheeled and soared and felt the rare privilege of flight. I wished Bill Riedesel and my old instructor, Eldon Hagen, could see me now. We rolled and flew on edge and slid down backward. The boilermaker went so well we did a second.

As I landed and taxied in, and the residual shame over the bent prop returned, I took what comfort I could from the applause.

The Carta Blanca people, prime sponsors of the race, had a big banquet planned for the evening. They invited everyone involved in Mexico's first "International Air Race," which was now completed without serious incident and considered by all to be a huge success.

Everyone received a certificate, a medal or a vote of thanks. Even the photographers were given awards, and each flashed a bulb at the crowd in appreciation. A special photographer covered the presentation with a four-light-bar Kodak movie outfit of a type common in the forties.

The Americano *pilotos* were in high humor, joking, toasting and arguing over the price of photos, taking sides as photographers wrestled for territory. Over it all rode the high notes of the trumpets from the Mariachi band.

I stepped outside to escape the racket. Although it was past ten P.M., the traffic was three abreast in both directions. Dust from the streets swirled about and mixed with barbeque smoke from street vendors' carts. Mexicali's atmosphere was unique.

We flew north the next morning. The air was moist, and Second Sweetheart's engine was running smoother than ever. But the smooth feel was misleading. At 2,550 rpms, the borrowed propeller's frequency exactly matched that of the engine rpm. Without my being aware of it, the specially shortened racing prop was vibrating in sympathy with the engine like a window might rattle at the passage of a heavy truck—ever so slightly, but ever so rapidly. In spite of the smooth engine sound, a fatal condition of resonance was building up.

Past Scipio, Utah, the ceilings lifted a bit and we rose to 400 feet. Now I noticed a mild vibration and tried to coax it out with small changes in throttle and mixture, climbing while I experimented, just in case the problem might be serious. I continued to climb as I checked the magnetos and fiddled with the mixture control, but nothing seemed to influence the rate or intensity of the vibration.

Suddenly, at 1,400 feet, the engine seemed to explode! And then the engine threatened to shake itself loose. My vision blurred as the entire plane shook violently. The spinner bobbed up and down in front of the nose. My hand was on the throttle and I instantly yanked it back. The pounding slowed, but every jolting vibration became more severe. Maps, a cap and objects too blurry to identify flew overboard. Quickly I turned off the magnetos and pulled up the nose, slowing the plane, hoping to stop the propeller from windmilling. When it finally stopped rotating, the reason for the vibration became obvious. One blade of the prop was missing—broken cleanly off about a foot from the hub!

There was a sudden quiet—a quiet that I had experienced before. It carried the same urgent message: The plane must be brought down now! Another forced landing—another unsolicited challenge.

The highway below was crowded with cars. For a moment I panicked, but the feeling passed and I stook stock. We still had 1,200 feet and the Sweetheart was gliding beautifully. I tightened the shoulder straps, unlatched my number two belt, checked my helmet strap and unplugged the radio jacks: I might want to get out fast. While I worked, I scanned the country for flat spots. A pasture directly below looked pretty good, but it was short and the north end was blocked by a transmission line. I glided east half a mile to check on a plowed field. Snow filled the furrows and the furrows ran crossways to the landing path. Enough looking! I headed back for the pasture, assuming the wind that blew the tumbleweed earlier still prevailed. Snow speckled the sky ahead with large flakes. Idiotically, I thought for a moment that I should delay landing until visibility improved; then I realized that I had no such choice. One way or another we would be on the ground in a matter of seconds.

Gliding downwind, parallel to my intended landing path, I searched for ditches and obstacles. The cow pies looked uniformly sprinkled, offering a faint hope of level land. I turned on base leg just after passing the power lines. Then, as altitude dwindled, I banked left, slipping over the wires in a hard turn, raising the nose to kill the speed, watching the airspeed needle hover on 100, then 90. Ten feet over the ground we were still traveling at 85, and the far fence was looming. I kicked rudder hard right, then left, barndooring the fuselage against the breeze. We thumped down, tail wheel first, then the main wheels, brakes full on. She was still light, and the skidding wheels had little effect. A large fallen tree trunk with scraggling branches raced by on the left. The fence grew large ahead, and I stood on the brakes, easing a bit at each tail bob. Each time the tail rose, the fence grew bigger. I considered a ground loop, but we miraculously slowed and coasted to a magnificent stop 20 yards short of the fence.

I looked into the gently falling snow that splattered the cockpit and said out loud, "Thanks, Boss!"

I sat in the plane marveling at my luck, and shamefully congratulating myself on the landing. But there were a few things I should have done that I didn't do: I should have radioed a quick "May Day"; I should have considered jumping—and above all, I should have shut off the fuel valve.

Second Sweetheart appeared to be intact everywhere except from the firewall forward. What used to be a neat assemblage of tubes and wires now looked like spaghetti. The engine mount was broken in two places, and the cowling was battered and bent from the engine's smashing against the sides of the compartment. The engine itself now sagged, pointing half-way to the ground, held in place only by the cowling and safety cable. The 3/16" steel safety cable, required for racing, had done its job. Had the engine broken loose, the aircraft would have been completely uncontrollable.

Up front, the broken propeller told its own story. The stub

showed two kinds of fracture. A thin break along the back side, brought on by resonance fatigue, had let the blade bend forward into the airstream—that was the mild vibration I had felt. The rest of the fracture showed signs of an instantaneous separation. That was the loud bang. The broken blade had flown off, to land perhaps a mile away. The unbalanced prop had caused the engine mount to break at the same instant.

Three propellers! In less than a week I had creamed three propellers—made modern works of art out of two, and broken the third clean off! How would I explain that to my wife, my fellow pilots or the insurance company?

Half a mile away, dimly visible through the snow shower, stood a farmhouse.

Neither Mrs. Hall nor her twelve-year-old son, Kurt, had heard me land, which was understandable, since the engine was silent. I called Jay first, and then the local sheriff. It was a difficult accident to explain, since all the damage had occurred in the air.

Young Kurt Hall and I walked back to the plane, pushed it to the fence and tied it down securely. The loose gear and baggage was all packed and stacked by the time the deputy sheriff and a newsman arrived. The story got on the wire service and it was so mixed up by the time it hit the home town media that close friends thought I had been either killed or badly hurt.

I began the long process of reporting the accident and planning the haul home. After repeating the date several times to the various officials, it dawned on me that January 9 was my fifty-fifth birthday. What a birthday present, but at least I was alive to contemplate another birthday.

The insurance company instructed me to hire a guard, and agreed to send an insurance adjuster to Salt Lake City in three days if we could have the plane dismantled and hauled that distance that soon.

The next evening Jay and my son, Wade, arrived, laden with packing materials, tools and a flatbed trailer in tow. By noon the next day we had the wings off and the entire craft secured for travel.

We met the insurance adjuster at the Salt Lake City Airport three days later. He stepped off an airliner, checked the plane, photographed it and filled out the necessary forms, then took the next flight out. We began the long gloomy drive back to Casper.

I can't remember ever having been more downcast. The damage was more extensive even than I had imagined. Suspicious wrinkles in the fuselage fabric near the tail meant that if the plane were ever to fly again all the covering would have to be stripped off and each tube and fitting minutely inspected. From the firewall forward, everything would have to be new: new mount, new engine, and, of course, new propeller. My beautiful little Starduster—and part of my life—was in ruins. It was as if my dream had come full circle and I had returned to the point where it all began.

Once again the Starduster stood in the driveway in front of my house. The late afternoon sunlight gleamed on her polished wings and on the shiny new black-and-white checkerboard paint job that decorated her nose. She had never looked more handsome. She was a show plane now, and as I stood gazing at her, it seemed to me that I had never felt such affection.

It had taken me six gruelling months of labor to bring her to this moment. For a while after the accident in Utah, I had been so discouraged that I could barely bring myself to look at the wreckage of Second Sweetheart. But dreams are not so easily killed. In time, almost imperceptibly, my thoughts began to turn to the possibility of repair. If I were to try to rebuild her, perhaps this time I could alter the elevator trim so as to get better control redundance, and move the static stick position forward to solve the "stick-up-the-leg" problem. Maybe I could find a more powerful engine, and maybe install those inverted fuel and oil systems I'd always wanted. Maybe I could even add a smoke-making device that would mark the path of our maneuvers with a white puffy tail. Maybe . . . .

When I finally did set to work, the task seemed almost overwhelming. The entire fuselage would have to be stripped, inspected, repaired and recovered. The fuel system would have to be completely reworked. New inspection holes would have to be cut in both wings and the spars carefully inspected. The new

170

engine would need a whole new mount, and that would have to be jigged and built from scratch. I'd have to cut and install a new firewall before the new cowling could be patterned. And so on and on.

Yet by the time the first weld was completed, I found myself beyond the point of drawing back. Once again I was firmly in the grip of my old dream—or obsession, if you will—and I could think of nothing but the day when the Starduster and I would take to the air again.

Now, six months later, that day was nearly here. I thought about the new engine—20 percent more powerful than the old one—about the new carburetor and oil system that would operate as well upside down as right side up, about the smoke-maker, about the dozens of other refinements, big and little, that I had added. The night would pass slowly as I reviewed and re-reviewed in my imagination the state of every vital fitting, every lock nut and safety. It would be another sleepless night.

At dawn the caravan would form and the Starduster would be towed to the airport. Perhaps to some casual bystanders she would seem unimpressive—merely a rather old-fashioned airplane rolling awkwardly, tail high and backward, down the highway. But to one fifty-five-year-old schoolteacher, she would be much more. In a few hours she would again become a magic steed, the Rosinante who could carry its rider back into a shining world filled with endless rows of windmills.